MARTIN

MARTIN LUTHER KING:
The Man
Who Could Not Hate

Mary Drewery

Marshalls

Marshalls
Lakeland/Oliphants
Samuel Bagster & Sons Ltd
Marshall Morgan & Scott
3 Beggarwood Lane, Basingstoke, Hants., UK.

ISBN 0 551 01104 1

Printed in Great Britain by
Richard Clay (The Chaucer Press) Ltd,
Bungay, Suffolk.

Contents

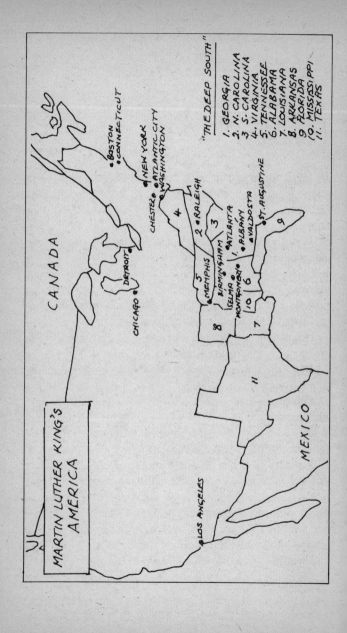

MARTIN LUTHER KING'S
AMERICA

CANADA

MEXICO

LOS ANGELES

CHICAGO

DETROIT

BOSTON
CONNECTICUT

NEW YORK

CHESTER
ATLANTIC-CITY
WASHINGTON

RALEIGH

MEMPHIS
BIRMINGHAM
SELMA
MONTGOMERY

ATLANTA
ALBANY
VALDOSTA

ST. AUGUSTINE

"THE DEEP SOUTH"

1. GEORGIA
2. N. CAROLINA
3. S. CAROLINA
4. VIRGINIA
5. TENNESSEE
6. ALABAMA
7. LOUISIANA
8. ARKANSAS
9. FLORIDA
10. MISSISSIPPI
11. TEXAS

1. The Shadow

In 1937, a clergyman took his eight-year-old son into a shop to buy him some new shoes. The shop assistant refused to serve them unless they moved to the back of the shop, out of sight of the other customers.

'We'll either buy shoes sitting here,' retorted the clergyman 'or we won't buy any shoes at all.'

The assistant was unmoved. With that, father and son marched out of the shop, the father muttering 'I don't care how long I have to live with this system, I am never going to accept it. I'll oppose it until the day I die.'

The same clergyman, driving his son home, was stopped by a traffic policeman.

'Boy,' the policeman addressed him arrogantly, 'I want to see your driving licence.'

The clergyman corrected the policeman courteously but firmly.

'*That* is a boy,' he said, indicating the lad in the front passenger seat. '*I* am a *man*.'

The setting for both these incidents was the city of Atlanta, Georgia, U.S.A. – the 'capital' of America's Deep South. The clergyman was the Reverend Martin Luther King, Senior, minister of Ebenezer Church, the largest and most important Baptist church in the city. He was always known affectionately as 'Daddy' King. The small boy was Martin Luther King, Junior, known at that time to his family as 'Mike'.

The reason for the incidents was that the Reverend King and his son were black, whereas the shop assistant and the traffic policeman were white. The two white men considered themselves superior to the Reverend King and, therefore, at liberty to insult him, even though he was a prosperous and respected member of the negro community.

It was no new thing for young Martin to be humiliated by white Americans. Even at the age of six, he had found himself forbidden any longer to associate with two little white boys who had until beginning school been his cherished playmates. Now they attended a white Elementary School, he a black. They could not mix. His mother grieved at his hurt bewilderment.

'Don't let it get you down,' she comforted him. 'Don't let it make you feel you're not as good as white people. You're as good as anyone else, and don't you forget it.'

But it was all too easy to forget that he was 'as good as anyone else', even though his parents were among Atlanta's black professional class; even though he lived in a spacious house with a garden in the part of Atlanta that housed the city's 'black élite'. It was all too easy to forget he was 'as good as anyone else' when a white woman he had never seen before walked up to him in an Atlanta department store and slapped his face. 'The little nigger stepped on my foot,' she announced to the world at large, even though Martin had been nowhere near her. The shadow of 'trouble' – that is, the white man – always lay across his world, no matter how faintly. He must also have been aware of, even if he did not understand, the threatening telephone calls and abusive letters his father received for his uncompromising stand on racial issues.

Much as these things hurt, however, they were only a

small part of young Martin's childhood. Secure in the love of his parents and the affection of his younger brother and sister; enjoying the material comforts of his well-appointed home, Martin grew into a sturdy, healthy lad. He was a good swimmer, tennis player and wrestler, a member of the neighbourhood baseball and football teams. At school he could take care of himself in an argument. 'Let's go to the grass', he would say – and that meant fighting it out.

Competent as he was with his fists, however, Martin soon discovered an even better way of settling a quarrel – with words. At quite an early age, after hearing a particularly moving sermon in church, Martin had told his mother: 'Some day I'm going to have me some big words like that.' After all, both his father and his maternal grandfather had been Baptist ministers and, from his earliest years, he had sat through the long, emotional sermons that were part of the negro Baptist tradition. He had joined in the joyful religious songs of southern negro Christians and their rhythms had become part of his being.

Inevitably, with such a background, his upbringing was strict and pious. He was reared in a tradition of hard work, thrift, service and responsibility. Days began and ended with family prayers. The three King children were required to learn verses of the Bible by heart and to be prepared to recite them at the evening meal table.

Even at an early age, Martin displayed a nature that swung between the poles of self-control and extreme emotionalism. When Daddy King used a cane to discipline his sons, Martin bore his punishment without so much as a protest or a whimper. On the other hand, when he felt that his 'sin' had caused his grandmother's death from a heart attack, he flung himself in despair out of an upstairs window, fortunately to no ill effect. Yet all the 'sin' the twelve-year-old boy had committed was to watch a parade on a Sunday!

This same year, 1941, the Kings moved to an even finer house at 193 Boulevard and Martin, the six years of his Elementary (or Junior) schooling behind him, began to attend the Booker T. Washington High School. This was the first public school for negro boys. Martin's grandfather, a founder member of the NAACP (National Association for the Advancement of Coloured People) had campaigned in the early twenties for its foundation. It was named after the great Negro leader and ex-slave who had urged that only through education would the negro develop sufficient influence to redress the inequality of his position in American society.

Like most schoolboys, Martin was keen to earn extra pocket money. He took on a paper round but, unlike many boys of his age who would spend their earnings on comics and sweets, Martin spent all his earnings on clothes. He always wanted to appear smart and favoured the well-shined patent leather shoes that were the height of fashion for young negroes at that time. Perhaps his fastidiousness over his appearance was linked with his awareness of his coloured skin. White Americans in the south kept themselves strictly apart from blacks. They tended to dismiss all negroes of whatever class (and there was a wealthy negro middle and professional class in Atlanta) as 'dirty niggers'. As a result, Martin was, all his life, obsessional about personal cleanliness. Whatever he was doing and no matter how busy or demanding his day, he was always immaculately turned out, his linen impeccable, his shoes gleaming, his whole person shining with health and cleanliness.

At High School, he took up the violin and piano, to add

to his other accomplishments. Inevitably, with his mastery of words, he became outstanding in debate, winning one of the school's annual prizes for oratory with a speech on 'The Negro and the Constitution'. He was already a deep-thinking boy, years ahead of his peers in his mental development. All of which, of course, made him resent the more deeply the insults heaped upon his race.

On one occasion, he and his school team had gone to take part in an inter-school debate in Valdosta, a town some two hundred miles from Atlanta, almost on the border with Florida. They were travelling back by coach but, when the bus stopped half-way home to take on more passengers, they were compelled to surrender their seats to whites. Never mind that their seats were booked for the whole two hundred miles – and there was no question of their being allowed to make a courteous gesture of *offering* their seats – instead, they were sworn at by the bus driver and made to stand in the aisle for the remaining hundred miles of the drive.

'It was a night I'll never forget,' Martin would later tell a correspondent from *Time* magazine. 'I don't think I have ever been so deeply angry in my life.'

Even in his 'teens, Martin was aware of the shameful fact that, in the middle of the twentieth century, the citizens of the United States could feel justified in humiliating, oppressing and constantly cursing one tenth of their number. The twenty-one million negroes in America were all descendants of the four million or more slaves brought from Africa during the 17th and 18th centuries to do unskilled heavy work on the newly settled southern plantations, work which in so hot a climate was too hard for white men. The 'triangular trade' out of Bristol and Liverpool made many Englishmen rich in those uncaring days. Gin and cheap finery were taken from England to the West coast of Africa where they were exchanged for negro slaves. These in turn were shipped to America and, with the proceeds of their sale, the traders bought sugar and tobacco and cotton which could be sold at a handsome profit back home.

When the American Declaration of Independence was drawn up in 1776 during the War of Independence against England, the negro part of the population seemed somehow to be forgotten. The Declaration stated that 'all men are created equal, that they are endowed by their Creator with certain unalienable rights, that among these are Life, Liberty, and the pursuit of Happiness.' Many Negroes must have felt it was a pity that their forebears were not considered 'equal' enough to share these benefits by being granted the right to vote! Perhaps the Founding Fathers of the United States had still looked on them as chattels.

Martin was born in 1929 – on 15th January – so he would have been fifteen and a half in the summer of 1944 when, for the first time, he went north with his brother, 'A.D.'. They had taken a vacation job on a tobacco farm in Connecticut, a New England state north of New York. The northern United States had, of course, fought the Confederate States of the South in the American Civil War of 1861 to 1865. Georgia, North and South Carolina, Virginia, Tennessee, Alabama, Louisiana, Arkansas, Florida, Mississippi, Texas – these eleven states all wanted to retain slavery which had been abolished in the north from 1776 onwards. They had been prepared to separate themselves from the rest of the Union and to have their own President. The North had won the war and, in theory at least, negroes everywhere were free and equal with whites. The South, however, still enforced strict segregation – that is, no mixing or sharing at all between white and black members of the community and, particularly, no vote for the negro. There was, in fact, still discrimination between black and white in the north as well, particularly over wages, but to the impressionable fifteen-year-old, used to the hostile atmosphere of the South where bitter memories of the war nourished hatred and contempt for the negro, the freedom of movement he enjoyed in New England and the casual friendliness of the whites he encountered seemed new heaven indeed.

In the south, he could not sit in a snack bar with whites; he could not use the same lavatories as whites; he could not enter swimming pools or parks used by whites; he was often denied public transport, even when there were vacant seats, if those seats were in the 'whites only' section. In fact, a young black only felt secure within the boundaries of his black 'ghetto'. He might have a fine house, a car, schools, banks, lawyers, churches, but they were all run *by* negroes *for* negroes. There was never any question of working, worshipping, learning, eating, least of all socialising alongside the white citizens of the south. All institutions combined to ensure that the negro remained a second-class citizen. In the north, black and white might not exactly love one another but they walked next to each other, sat next to each other, talked to each other.

So the freedom of that summer of 1944 must have been a revelation to young Martin. To be able to hold up his head proudly and not be made to feel inferior must have reinforced the assurances his mother had given him so many years before: 'You're as good as anyone else, and don't you forget it.'

Thus, it must have seemed even more humiliating than usual when Martin entered the dining-car of the train back to Atlanta, to have to eat in a curtained-off section (known as a 'Jim Crow' car) lest his presence offend the white diners. And this train was starting its journey in the north! It was a shattering blow to his self-esteem.

Martin admitted later that, during his 'teens, he came as near to hating white people as at any time in his life. But, passionately as he already felt about the injustices heaped upon his race, he was already mature enough to realise that hatred was an unworthy and poisonous emotion. Hatred could only breed violence and more hatred. There must be a better way.

Finding that better way would have to wait, though. After his return from the north, all his energies had to be directed towards gaining entry to Morehouse, the 'black' College at which 'Daddy' King had been educated.

2.   College Boy

Dr. Benjamin Mays, the distinguished President of Morehouse, was seriously concerned at the falling intellectual standard of the intake into his college. Segregated schools set a limit on the standard of teaching and competition among students. In a fair society, the best of negro *and* white brains should be in competition to bring out the best of both. As it was, black schools with black teachers had, for the most part, a much lower standard than white schools. Moreover, the Second World War was still raging and conscription into the army was taking promising youngsters at just the time when they would normally be enrolling at University. To combat these problems, Dr. Mays started a special programme to attract exceptionally gifted High School students to Morehouse.

Young Martin, being so gifted, had already jumped two classes at High School. Now he passed the necessary examinations and was accepted at Morehouse in September 1944 when he was only fifteen. Normally, he would have needed to be eighteen to enter college. He must have been exceptionally clever.

Daddy King was delighted. It was his hope that, just as Martin had followed him to Morehouse, so he would follow him into the ministry. The idea did not appeal to Martin. He did not like the highly emotional tradition of the southern negro church. He was embarrassed by the hand-clapping, the stamping, the shouting aloud, the 'Amen'-ing at the services. He considered most of its ministers un-intellectual and untrained – perhaps a supercilious view for a fifteen-year-old to take but perhaps he was a bit of an intellectual snob at this time. In any case, he had set his heart on medicine as a career.

He now had to adapt to the high standards set by the college. At all times the students were exhorted to conduct themselves 'like Morehouse men' – in other words, to try their best to achieve excellence in the belief that only by education would the negro be able to overcome the handicap of his colour in the hostile white world outside. It was Booker T. Washington's creed worked out in practice.

College life was very high-powered for a fifteen-year-old. At first, much of the course was beyond Martin – classes in philosophy are hard-going at the best of times! It provided a much-needed lesson in humility. However, quite early on, Thoreau's essay 'On Civil Disobedience' moved him with an intensity that would colour his approach to the Civil Rights campaigns of his later years.

At the same time as learning to cope with the faster intellectual pace of Morehouse, the precocious boy was developing into a personable young man. Though stockily built and of only medium height, Martin was agile and athletic. He had great personal charm of character and his wit and eloquence made him irresistable to the girls of Atlanta's black upper class. Someone said of him: 'Mike King played hard, dressed well, and attempted to be a great lover.'! But it was all part of growing up.

Greater maturity brought with it, too, the realisation that medicine was not the right course of study. Martin's temperament yearned for human problems rather than scientific, so he decided to specialise in sociology. This would qualify him for law school and, with his natural gift for oratory and debate, he looked all set for a successful career in the legal profession.

One of his teachers at college, Professor Walter Chivers, impressed upon his young coloured students that the biggest evil they had to overcome in society was racism – that is, the assumption by white people that, by virtue only of being white, they could consider themselves superior to people with coloured skins. In the old days, some white children were told by their parents that negroes were created by God especially to serve white people and their skins were black because they were full of sin! Martin's generation found racism most clearly illustrated in the economic system.

This truth was soon demonstrated to Martin in the vacation jobs he took with white firms in Atlanta – with the Railway Express and with the Southern Springs Bed Mattress Company. Most American college students, boys and girls, help to maintain themselves during their four years at college by doing paid jobs, as waiters, unskilled labourers, 'home-helps' and the like during the long summer vacation. Martin found the experience shattering. He discovered that regular black workers, not just students, were subjected to conditions of appalling degradation. Their wages were far less than those of whites doing the same work. They were constantly abused by their white employers and, worst of all, could be dismissed without notice, even after years of faithful service.

When a Railway Express foreman called him 'nigger', Martin promptly left the job of his own accord. But the experience caused him to think deeply about the negro's lot in society. Martin's family enjoyed financial independence so he could afford to give in his notice. But what if he had been entirely dependent on that job to pay his college fees, or even for his very existence? What if he had had a family to support? In that case, he, like the majority of negroes would have had to learn to put up with the insults in order to keep his job. He would have had to live in constant fear of losing his livelihood if he were not sufficiently servile. Martin began to realise how privileged he was among the negro community and of how much self-confidence he had acquired through being a student of Morehouse. He realised that the training had made him afraid of nothing and nobody. It was the best preparation he could have had for the life that lay ahead of him.

If it had not been for the college's building up of each student's self-confidence, it would have been easy to develop a hatred of whites, but through the college Martin met students from white colleges in Atlanta. The meetings reassured him. He discovered that all whites were not racist – indeed, that many white students thought as he did about the evils of racism. No doubt, also, the Christian truths which he had absorbed from his earliest years could not help making themselves felt. He found he could not hate.

Consideration of right and wrong was of great importance to him. Indeed, he felt it should be an integral part of education. He wrote an article for the Morehouse College magazine in which he declared that education which was only concerned with efficiency could be a menace to society. He pointed out that an educated man with no sense of right or wrong could turn into a dangerous criminal. Education should provide men with 'noble ends', rather than means to an end.

Slowly, forces were at work prompting him, nudging him, gently moving him towards his real vocation. It was increasingly borne in upon Martin that the law was no more the career for him than was medicine – it must be the ministry. So for the third time, he changed the course of his studies and in June 1948, at the age of only nineteen, he received his Bachelor's degree from Morehouse College and was named co-pastor of his father's church where he had been ordained the year before.

3. Interlude

Martin's ordination was the realisation of Daddy King's dreams. Now, surely, the boy would become full-time co-pastor with him of Ebenezer Baptist Church. Martin had already preached a trial sermon there with great success.

Wisely, Martin decided that he needed more experience. Apart from vacation jobs, he had never lived away from home. Moreover, if he was going to be what he would call a 'trained' minister, he needed to achieve more advanced degrees.

He enrolled at Crozer Theological Seminary in Chester, Pennsylvania, for a three-year course to take the degree of Bachelor of Divinity. This was an 'integrated' college – that is, it admitted both white and black students – so at last Martin had the experience of studying alongside whites. He was one of only six negro students out of a hundred at Crozer so felt himself very much 'on trial'. In the event, he showed up very well against the white competition, excelling in Bible criticism, church history and administration, and in practice preaching.

At first, he was intensely serious, punctual and, inevitably, neat. He had no desire to match the white stereotype of the negro as always late, always loud and laughing, of being dirty and messy. However, as he gained confidence at Crozer, he made many friends among his white fellow-students – although there were the usual tensions he had come to expect.

'Room raids' by students were a common prank and were usually accepted as good fun. One white student from North Carolina, however, re-acted violently when his room was raided. Although Martin had not taken part in this particular raid, the North Carolina student threatened him with a pistol. The crisis blew over when the other students disarmed him and eventually he and Martin became firm friends but it made Martin wary of his white fellows. They were on occasion distant towards the six coloured students so the negroes, for their part, turned to each other for friendship.

Martin found a 'home-from-home' with the Reverend J. Pius Barbour who was minister of the nearest Baptist church. Martin would join them for supper after service. Mrs. Barbour was a splendid cook and her steak served in a rich, spicy sauce, reminded Martin of home. He was always interested in food and called it his 'besetting sin'.

The Divinity Course at Crozer was high-powered. Martin plunged into a study of philosophy, both ancient and modern. He learned about great figures in Christianity and in other religions. He was particularly impressed when he learned of the campaign of non-violence conducted in India by Mahatma Gandhi. After attending a lecture on his travels in India by the President of Howard University, Martin was so inspired by what he heard of Gandhi's spiritual leadership and his pacifist methods that he went straight from the meeting to buy as many books as he could find on Gandhi's life and works. He learned from them that true pacifism was not just giving way but courageously confronting evil with love and being prepared to suffer violence rather than inflict it on anyone else. At all times, good should be returned for evil. Gandhi might have been a Hindu but his teaching was Christ's:

> 'But what I tell you is this: Do not set yourself against the man who wrongs you. If someone slaps you on the right cheek, turn and offer him your left. If a man wants to sue you for your shirt, let him have your coat as well . . . Love your enemies and pray for your persecutors . . .'
>
> (Matt. 5.39–45)

Martin's studies demanded hard work and concentration. He was also preaching regularly, and with growing confidence, at local churches – but the young dandy of Atlanta and the Romeo of Morehouse still found time to pay court to a number of girls at once during his limited spare time – so much so that at his graduation, *several* claimed to be his fiancée! However, none of these relationships was serious except one.

During the third year of Martin's course when, unusually for a negro, he was elected President of the student body, Martin met and fell deeply in love with a white girl, the daughter of one of the College staff. Despite the fact that Crozer was a Christian theological college, the brotherhood of man was not entirely subscribed to. Racial prejudice lurked just below the surface. The romance could only be doomed to failure in such circumstances. The Reverend Barbour used the weight of his office to warn the young people of the difficulties that would lie ahead if they persisted in their relationship. Reluctantly, they agreed to go their separate ways and Martin never again allowed himself to become emotionally involved with a white woman.

The problem was highlighted shortly afterwards when

Martin and a friend took two girls to a restaurant in the small New Jersey village of Maple Shade near Camden. The waiters repeatedly ignored Martin's request for the menu and eventually the white proprietor of the restaurant suggested that they should leave. Martin refused; after all, the State laws permitted 'integrated' restaurants. In a rage, the proprietor produced a pistol and threatened to shoot the four students if they did not leave immediately. They left, the girls terrified. Half an hour later, Martin and his friend returned with a police officer who took statements from three white students in the restaurant to the effect that the proprietor had indeed threatened Martin and his friends, had refused to serve them and had so violated the Civil Rights Code of the State of New Jersey. Triumphantly, Martin turned over the case to the NAACP for them to file a suit in the courts against the restaurant proprietor. But it was all a waste of effort. When it came to appearing in court, the three witnesses refused to give evidence. They claimed they could not remember the details of the incident. It was another triumph for white racism – and for Martin, another confrontation with evil. He had tried to combat it through legal means and had failed. He had not yet sufficient maturity to try love – but he knew that racism was an evil that he would have to confront and conquer – some day.

Meantime, he concentrated on his work and in June, 1951 graduated as Bachelor of Divinity with top marks for his year. He was honoured by being invited to deliver the valedictory address at the degree ceremony. He was awarded the Pearl M. Plafker citation for being the most outstanding student; he was granted the J. Lewis Crozer fellowship of $1,300 to pursue further graduate studies.

His proud parents gave him a green Chevrolet car – and

at twenty-two, Bachelor of Divinity or not – one's first car is a landmark in life!

Throughout 1952, the green Chevvy was regularly parked in Massachussetts Avenue, Boston, outside the apartment Martin shared with his former Morehouse friend, Philip Lenud. Martin had moved to Boston in September 1951 when he enrolled at the University as a candidate for the degree of Doctor of Philosophy. Parallel with his studies at Boston, Massachussetts, he was also taking philosophy courses at Harvard, a few miles away at Cambridge.

The apartment was immediately opposite the Savoy Ballroom where College dances took place most evenings, but neither young negro dared to attend – it would be humiliating to be refused entry. Instead, they frequented the Totem Pole, a lively nightclub catering for negroes, or else they would eat at Mrs. Jackson's Western Lunch Box where Martin could satisfy his craving for highly spiced Southern-style food.

He was missing the South, despite its indignities – and not just the food and the climate. He found Boston girls reserved and was lonely for the many girl friends he had had at home. So when a friend gave him the telephone number of a Miss Coretta Scott, a Southern girl studying music at the New England Conservatory in Boston but hailing from the southern state of Alabama, he was eager to arrange a meeting.

Coretta, apparently, considered his approach somewhat brash. He said something over the telephone to the effect that he was 'like Napoleon at Waterloo before her charms' to which she replied crisply that he had not seen her yet! She agreed reluctantly to a meeting and, such was her impact on Martin, that he proposed marriage on their very first date!

He was not accepted immediately. Coretta was dedicated to her career as a singer and did not want to give it up. Moreover, she and Martin had totally different attitudes to racism.

Coretta was the daughter of a prosperous family in Marion, Alabama. Her father had struggled hard to maintain his independence and, by the end of World War II, he owned a garage and petrol station, a haulage firm, a chicken farm and a large grocery store. His work brought him into competition with whites who resented his success and threatened him. The Scott family believed in taking action when they encountered racial prejudice and Coretta supported this attitude. She always said that she would only marry a man who was highly intelligent *and* a Civil Rights 'activist'.

Martin certainly filled the former of these requirements but he was by temperament and by passionate belief committed to a non-violent approach to the black man's struggle to obtain his Civil Rights. It was by no means a cowardly attitude. It takes more courage to remain calm and to show love when provoked than to strike back; and Martin's ideas of non-violence arose from a deep spiritual conviction, a profound love of Christ and His message.

So there were differences in temperament to be overcome between Martin and Coretta, as well as the pull of their respective careers. Daddy King was strongly opposed to the match. Prosperous though Coretta's background was, her social status in the black community was not what Daddy King looked for in a daughter-in-law; nor had she particular beauty or poise. He would have preferred Martin to choose an Atlanta girl with good social connections. Martin was adamant. Coretta had all that he was looking for in a wife and they loved one another. His view prevailed and they were married on 18th June, 1953 in the garden of Coretta's home in Alabama. Daddy King performed the ceremony.

The young couple returned to Boston for them both to complete their courses. Martin had in addition to finish the thesis for his doctorate, which was on a very abstruse theological subject. They had to decide where they were going to live after college and what Martin should do. He had taken one higher degree and had almost completed a second. It was necessary now to begin to earn a living.

Of course, once again Daddy King offered a joint pastorate at Ebenezer Church in Atlanta but Martin and Coretta wanted to be on their own at the start of their married life together. Martin had firm offers of pastorates at two churches in the North and from two in the South. He was offered a deanship (that is, an administrative post in a college) and teaching posts in three other colleges but he felt he ought to have experience in a church before shutting himself away in an academic career. Coretta wanted him to take one of the Northern churches but Martin was missing the south.

In December 1953, he preached a 'trial sermon' at Dexter Avenue Baptist Church, Montgomery, Alabama. It must have impressed the church for he was invited to accept the pastorate. Although it was a black church in a southern city, Dexter Avenue church had a distaste for emotionalism and 'amen'-ing in the services. It had an educated, well-heeled congregation who were looking for an intelligent minister. This combination of 'intellectual' church and southern setting was everything Martin could have wished for.

He accepted the pastorate and travelled regularly from Boston to Montgomery each weekend until Coretta completed her course in the summer of 1954. That August they moved to Montgomery and settled down in their first real home. Like most newly-married couples, they were looking forward to a peaceful period when they could grow together in love, could build up their position in the church, and start a family. Both had twenty years of study behind them and, although they knew that the church was a demanding vocation, they would no longer be burdened with examinations. Martin's thesis reached the required standard and he was awarded his Doctorate in June 1955. He settled down well in the church and was extremely popular. A baby daughter, Yolande Denise (or Yoki, as she was known) was born on 17th November of that year. All seemed set for a happy and peaceful time.

But it was not to be.

On Thursday, December 1st, 1955, a quiet, respectable middle-aged negro woman went Christmas shopping in Montgomery and thereafter life for the Martin Luther Kings would never be the same again.

4. Boycott

December 1st, 1955 had been a cold day with drizzle. Even so, the shops had been crowded and now, in the early evening, weary shoppers laden with parcels, office workers anxious to get home made long queues at the bus stops. When Mrs. Rosa Parks at last reached the head of the queue in Court Square and boarded the bus, she settled down gratefully into a seat behind the white passengers for her journey home. She was a seamstress, a sweet-natured gentle woman, formerly employed by the local head of the NAACP.

The bus pulled up with a jerk at the next stop outside the Empire Theatre. Similarly burdened shoppers swarmed on, some of them white. The conductor pushed his way along the aisle. 'Move!' he ordered Mrs. Parks. 'You, nigger. Get to the back of the bus.'

Mrs. Parks looked up at him. 'No!' she said.

Again, she was ordered out of her seat. Again she refused – politely but firmly. It was not that she wanted to make an issue over civil rights. 'I was tired,' she explained later, 'and my feet hurt.'

Whatever the reason for her quiet refusal, it made no difference to the attitude of the conductor. He called the police and Mrs. Parks was arrested.

This caused outrage among the black community and, for once, the city authorities found themselves in a dilemma. Normally when a negro refused to move, there was an argument, maybe a punch-up, so that the victim could be charged with the loosely-defined offence of 'disorderly conduct'. That way, it was not easy to prove that the bus conductors were showing racial discrimination. But Mrs. Parks was so quiet and dignified that there was no possibility that a charge could be proved on that ground. Thus the authorities were compelled explicitly to charge her with the 'violation of the municipal ordinance governing racial accommodation on a publicly owned vehicle.' In other words, the authorities would have to admit publicly that they had racist policies and the Court would have to demonstrate that it upheld those policies.

This time the negro community decided that enough was enough. The clergy of three black Baptist churches – the Reverend Ralph Abernathy (who was Mrs. Parks' pastor); the Reverend E. D. Nixon and Martin – called upon all negroes to boycott the bus services of Montgomery on the day of Mrs. Parks' trial.

They held meetings on Friday evening, 2nd December. Over the weekend, forty thousand leaflets were distributed recommending and explaining the boycott. The Sunday sermons hammered home the message. Advertisements were placed in both black and white Sunday newspapers explaining why on the following day negroes would not be using the public bus services. 'Don't ride the bus to work, to town, to school or any place' was the message. Instead, taxi companies owned by negroes agreed to transport their fellow blacks for the same fare as they would have paid on the buses. Many would walk. Many would go by private car. Many with cars would offer lifts to those without transport.

It was not merely to be a demonstration of solidarity with Mrs. Parks; it would also affect the profits of the local bus company because negroes were the main users.

Although the negroes in Montgomery outnumbered the whites, they enjoyed few rights as citizens. Only two thousand of them had the vote out of fifty to sixty thousand. The bus companies were particularly cruel in their treatment of blacks. The negroes would have to pay their fares at the front of the bus but were then ordered to get off and board the bus from the rear into the 'Jim Crow' section. Before they could get aboard, however, the bus would often move off leaving them behind. The conductors were insulting, calling their negro passengers 'niggers', 'black apes' or 'black cows'. Bus drivers were armed and had even been known to kill black passengers out of hand.

On Monday morning, Martin and Coretta were up early, waiting for the first big orange bus of the day to go past their house at 6 o'clock. It was still dark so that the illuminated interior of the bus shone clearly as the vehicle approached. They could see the driver at the wheel and behind him – empty seats. There was not a single passenger on the bus!

Perhaps it was too early for passengers. Better not count on success yet.

They waited for the next bus – and the next. The pattern repeated itself. Then the telephone began to ring with news of the position on other routes. They were filled with elation. All over the city, it appeared, the boycott of the buses was almost one hundred per cent complete. For the first time, a negro protest was organised, fully supported and effective.

That Monday morning, Mrs. Parks appeared in court, was found guilty, fined ten dollars and ordered to pay costs. It was an unnecessarily hard penalty for having tired feet! Her solicitor immediately filed notice of appeal against the conviction.

At 3 o'clock that afternoon, the leaders of the black community met together and formed the Montgomery Improvement Association (the MIA) and, to his intense surprise, Martin found himself elected President. He was only twenty-six but already showed outstanding intelligence and force of character, and he had developed a reputation as a dynamic speaker. Moreover, the very fact that he was new to Montgomery was an asset in that he did not belong to any particular faction in the black community.

Events moved swiftly. On leaving the afternoon meeting he was told that in less than three hours he would be required to address a mass meeting at Holt Street Baptist Church. Less than three hours! He was used to spending fifteen hours in preparation for his normal Sunday sermon.

He hurried home to break the news to Coretta. What if she should object? But he had chosen the right wife. 'Whatever you do,' Coretta assured him, 'You have my backing.'

At a quarter to six, Martin left for the meeting. There had been no time to prepare an address, only to assemble his thoughts. His address would have to be militant enough to strengthen the resolve of the negroes but moderate enough to keep their fervour within bounds. He would have to speak without notes to the biggest congregation he had ever addressed. The number in the audience far exceeded expectations: four thousand people packed the church. There was a prayer, a short scripture reading, then the Vice-President of the MIA introduced the new young President.

The audience was quiet as Martin told the story of Mrs. Parks and as he catalogued the injustices perpetrated by the bus company. He talked about the boycott and urged:

'In spite of the mistreatment that we have confronted, we must not become bitter and end up hating our white brothers.'

Martin could feel the response of his audience as he warmed to his theme. His rich, deep, baritone voice took on a rhythmic cadence as he launched into his peroration:

'There comes a time when people get tired.
We are here this evening to tell those who have mistreated us so long that *we* are tired – tired of being segregated and humiliated; tired of being kicked about by the brutal feet of oppression.
We have no alternative but to protest.
We have sometimes given our white brothers the feeling that we liked the way we were being treated, but we have come here tonight to be saved from that patience that makes us patient with anything less than freedom and justice.'

No wonder his words brought a resounding 'Amen' from the audience.

The meeting voted overwhelmingly to continue the boycott of the buses so on Wednesday morning, December 7th, Martin called together the leaders of the MIA and other people prominent in the negro community to plan the strategy for a long campaign. There was one white on the Executive Committee, the Reverend Robert Graetz, President of the Alabama Human Relations Council.

By Thursday, December 8th, after only three days, the boycott was beginning to bite financially. Withdrawal of black passengers meant a 75% loss of revenue to the bus companies and the Montgomery City Line, for one, was already acutely embarrassed financially. The bus companies agreed to meet the black leaders.

Martin presented the three-point proposal agreed upon: first, negroes were to be treated with courtesy by the bus drivers; second, that bus seats should be filled on a 'first come, first served' basis, the blacks starting at the back and the whites from the front; third, that on mainly 'black' routes, negroes should be employed as drivers.

These demands were modest and reasonable enough but Montgomery was not a reasonable community. It considered itself above the law of the United States and bound only by its own local regulations. A month before the Rosa Parks incident, the Inter-State Commerce Commission had banned racial segregation on any form of transport between states, but Montgomery's buses had remained segregated. In fact, Montgomery was one of the worst cities in the south for racism. The average wage of the negro was half that of a white labourer. With the exception of a tiny black upper class – from whom the congregation of Martin's church were drawn – most negroes suffered appalling housing conditions. Less than one in three had flush loos. There were no recreation facilities for negroes, schools were inadequate and the white police were usually rude and brutal. There was so much that Martin would have liked to protest about but for the moment he was putting forward only the modest three-point proposal regarding buses.

It met with a hostile reception.

The lawyer for the bus company, Jack Crenshaw, declared that 'the blacks would go about boasting of the victory they had won over white people – and that they wouldn't stand for!' In vain did Martin promise that he would urge his people to contain their elation if the proposals were accepted, but it was no use. Other than a concession that the bus company would *try* to make their drivers more courteous, the answer to the proposals was 'No'. Moreover, a wily move by one of the Mayor's commissioners led to the revival of a municipal regulation which stipulated a *minimum* fare for all taxis. This meant that negro taxi drivers could no longer just charge the equivalent of a bus fare to their negro passengers; and those passengers could not afford the decreed minimum taxi fare.

After consideration, Martin and the committee countered by organising a car pool among negro car owners to give lifts instead of negroes having to use taxis. By the following evening, one hundred and fifty private cars were working from forty-eight despatch and forty-two collection points. The operation worked with almost military precision.

There was an added bonus that some of the wealthier negroes who never themselves used buses were able, through sharing their cars, to get to know poorer negroes and a bond became established between them. After a day or two, some white car owners joined the pool in sympathy with the black cause. The MIA committee had taken advertising space in white newspapers to set out their case and there were some white people in Montgomery who could see that the negro demands were fair and modest.

Many negroes chose to walk to work to demonstrate their commitment to the cause. One elderly negress, declining a lift, declared: 'I'm not walking for myself. I'm walking for my children and my grandchildren.'

The Montgomery bus boycott had become a crusade. Martin declared 'God has decided to use Montgomery as the proving ground for the struggle and triumph of freedom and justice in America.' But if triumph was to come, it would be proved through suffering and fire.

On the morning of 17th December there was a second meeting between the MIA, city officials and representatives of the bus companies. The meeting was no more successful than before and Martin was criticised publicly by a white minister for involving himself in civil rights issues. 'Salvation, not transportation, is the province of the pastor,' he was told. A third meeting two days later broke up after much acrimonious dispute. Martin was accused of 'intolerance and obduracy' because he refused to abandon the three point proposals.

The boycott continued. The bus companies continued to lose money. The white side became increasingly frustrated by the solidarity of the negro community. Extremist white elements began a series of threatening telephone calls to members of the Committee which caused fear, distress and, in one instance, a nervous breakdown. Four times the MIA was harassed into moving its headquarters until at last it found security in a negro-owned building.

The Montgomery City Lines were losing so much money through the boycott that they had to increase the fares charged to the few white citizens who used the buses. After a couple of months, businesses in Montgomery such as shops had lost over a million dollars in trade owing to the restricted movement of the black population. Various attempts were made to undermine the boycott. A fictitious announcement was made in the press that the boycott was over but Martin was warned in time and was able to circulate a note to the negro clergy asking them to refute the announcement in their Sunday sermons.

Unable to find a way out of the impasse by reasonable means, the extreme element of white Montgomery resorted to intimidation. Negroes were arrested at random on patently fabricated charges. Those waiting at the pick-up points for cars from the car-pool were arrested for 'vagrancy and illegal hitch-hiking'. Martin himself was arrested for alleged 'speeding'.

On the evening of 30th January, 1956, Martin's home was bombed.

He was out at the time at a meeting. Coretta was at home with a friend and ten-week-old Yoki. It can only have been God's providence that urged the two women to leave where they were in the front room of the house to go and look at the baby. Fractionally later, dynamite was tossed onto the front porch, blasting out the door and windows.

As the dust and noise of the explosion subsided, the telephone rang shrilly. Coretta lifted the receiver. A woman's voice, harsh with hatred, said 'I did it – and I'm only sorry I didn't kill all you bastards.'

A crowd swiftly collected outside the house and its mood was ugly. The police, who were white, arrived quickly on the scene. They were, as normally, armed – but some of the blacks were armed too. Martin, pushing his way in frantic anxiety through the police and firemen to his shattered front door heard one say 'All right. You've got your .38; I've got mine. Let's shoot it out.'

Still not knowing whether Coretta and the baby were safe, Martin sensed the tension and knew he must speak. He turned to the crowd and raised his hands for quiet.

'My friends,' he addressed the crowd. 'We believe in law and order. Don't get panicky. Don't get your weapons. He who lives by the sword will perish by the sword. Remember, that is what God said. We are not advocating violence. We want to love our enemies. We must love our white brothers no matter what they do.

I did not start this boycott. I was asked by you to serve

37

as your spokesman. I want it to be known the length and breadth of the land that if I am stopped, this movement will not stop. If I am stopped, our work will not stop, for what we are doing is right. What we are doing is just and God is with us.'

He waited anxiously as, one by one, the angry crowd pocketed their knives and pistols, dropped their stones, began to disperse. The police, too, lowered their weapons, went back to their cars and drove away. Someone called out 'God bless you, son!'. Only then dare Martin look for Coretta.

Blood letting had been avoided on that occasion but the bombings did not stop. Many of the black leaders had their homes attacked during the following days.

Martin took Coretta and the baby to Atlanta for a few days to recover from the shock. However, a telephone call from his friend Ralph Abernathy informed him that all the MIA leaders, including Martin, had been indicted for 'conspiracy to interfere with normal business'.

'I must go back at once to answer to the charge,' said Martin.

Daddy King begged him not to go. So did his mother. Even the MIA leaders in Montgomery added their voice but Martin was adamant. He would not desert his colleagues at such a time.

Daddy King drove him and Coretta back to Montgomery where, with Ralph, Martin reported to the County goal. The two ministers were charged, photographed and released on bail pending trial.

The 'mugshot' of the Reverend Dr. Martin Luther King, Jnr., ordained priest, albeit negro, with a numbered plaque (7089) hanging round his neck like a common criminal, a murderer or a rapist, appeared the following morning on the front page of every newspaper in the

United States – and protest and indignation were voiced from coast to coast.

5. Hollow Victory

Mahatma Gandhi was the inspiration of much of Martin Luther King's thinking, in particular his non-violent method of protest. At the time, the Martin-led Montgomery bus boycott was likened to Gandhi's famous 'salt march' to Dandi in 1930.

The events were similar in that both campaigns used an issue of relative unimportance to highlight much greater injustices. In Montgomery, the demand for 'courteous treatment' on buses, even for the right to seats, was nothing compared with the fundamental problem of the economic plight of and lack of franchise by the negro. In India, Gandhi defied the state monopoly on the production of salt (a staple commodity required by the poorest peasant) to challenge the British Government's treatment of the Indians under its rule. But whereas Gandhi and his followers deliberately broke what they considered an unjust law (that is, they used a campaign of *civil disobedience*), Martin was using the lawful means of a boycott in a campaign for civil rights.

At least, he thought the boycott was legal – until the Montgomery authorities managed to turn up some obscure law that the boycott could reasonably be argued to contravene!

Both in India and in Montgomery, arrests were made on a large scale. In India, 100,000 people were arrested and jailed, including Gandhi himself. In Montgomery, in a local as opposed to a national campaign, ninety-one negroes including Martin and all the other black clergy, were brought before the local court on 19th March, charged with 'hindering lawful business without just cause or excuse'.

The court was packed. Negro supporters overflowed the public benches. Many wore crosses or lapel badges with the words 'Father, forgive them'. Witness after witness testified to the harsh treatment negroes received on the buses. They cited instances where negro passengers had been shot dead by the bus driver simply for asking for the return of their fares when turned off the bus. It was all to no avail. The trial was not about the justice or injustice of a segregated bus service; the issue was whether the negroes had violated Alabama's state laws by their boycott. And, of course, *technically* it could be argued that they *had* 'hindered lawful business' in that they had caused the bus companies to lose money, even though they had every 'just cause or excuse' for so doing. But, faced with the prejudiced attitude of a Southern court, they did not stand a chance. All were convicted.

Martin was fined $500 and costs (with the option of 386 days' hard labour). This, he was graciously told, was a 'minimal' sentence owing to his 'pacific and responsible leadership'! Some of the others found guilty were not so 'fortunate'. Once again, Martin appealed against his conviction.

But at least the massive publicity given to the case was bringing Martin support on a national scale.

On 17th May, 1956 he was invited to speak at the Cathedral of St. John the Divine in New York. For Montgomery's problems to be considered worth discussing a thousand miles away was a moral triumph indeed.

Later that month, at a big rally in Madison Square Gardens in New York, famous speakers such as Eleanor Roosevelt (widow of the late President), Sammy Davis, Jnr. and Tallulah Bankhead raised much-needed funds as a practical contribution to the cause.

Despite this support, however, Martin was becoming depressed as the boycott dragged on through the long, hot summer months, with absolutely no sign of any agreement being reached. Sometimes he wondered just what else the Montgomery whites could think up to try to break the boycott. A new ploy came later in the year when the city declared the negroes' car pool both 'a public nuisance' and an 'unlicensed private enterprise'.

Martin was even more depressed when he learned that his appeal against his March conviction was to be heard on 13th November before Judge Carter, a known segregationist.

It seemed nothing less than a miracle that on the very day of the appeal, the United States Supreme Court decreed that Alabama's state and local laws requiring segregation on buses were unconstitutional. It was a resounding victory for the negro cause. Nevertheless, Judge Carter felt able to go against the spirit of the Federal decree by granting the city authorities an injunction against the negroes' car pool!

Federal law (this is, laws passed by Congress and upheld by the United States Supreme Court) should always supersede the laws of individual states but Montgomery's whites were not inclined to accept direction from the Supreme Court. On the night following the decree, members of the dreaded Ku Klux Klan took to the streets. This hateful secret society was founded in 1866 and aimed at intimidating negroes. Its members were disguised in long white robes. Their faces were hidden under tall pointed hoods with only slits for the eyes. They used as their symbol a fiery cross and were notorious for burning, whipping and lynching their victims.

This night, an awesome procession of forty vehicles filled with Klansmen drove through the black neighbourhoods of Montgomery. A year before, their appearance on the streets would have struck terror in the hearts of the negro population. This year, 1956, made confident by the Supreme Court's decision in their favour, the negroes faced the Klansmen without fear. They put the lights on in their houses, came out onto the pavements and lined the roadside, laughing at the sinister procession where once they would have screamed with terror and fled. The gesture of the Ku Klux Klan proved an empty threat. The forty vehicles put on speed and hurried away from the negro areas. In its way, this was an even greater psychological victory than had been the news of the Supreme Court's ruling.

This was November. The Federal Order, the actual piece of paper forbidding segregation on the buses would not reach Montgomery for another month – such are the slow processes of the law. So there was no change in the situation. The bus companies would not change their policy till the paper arrived so the boycott had to go on. In the meantime, Martin and his committee felt it advisable to obey the ruling of the local court. The car pool was disbanded and, though winter was once more upon them, negroes who could not afford taxis walked to work rather than break the boycott.

But it *would* end – as soon as the Federal Order arrived.

Then what would happen?

Martin and his committee were anxious that there should be no excuse for any kind of violence. Martin urged the negroes not to triumph openly at the success of their

44

campaign and he began a programme of mass teaching of the tactics of peaceful resistance.

Sessions in the churches were given over to lectures on non-violence. Sometimes, little scenes were acted out with some negroes pretending to be abusive whites, others acting as themselves and trying to respond in a dignified and Christian manner. The MIA sent out a circular to all negro homes setting out the behaviour they should observe:

'If cursed, do not curse back,' it read. 'If struck, do not strike back, but evidence love and goodwill at all times.

If another person is being molested, do not arise to go to his defence, but pray for the oppressor.'

This was the Sermon on the Mount translated into twentieth century terms. Martin and his committee hoped that by setting an example themselves, they could carry their fellow negroes with them – and to a very large extent they succeeded.

On 20th December, 1956 the Federal Order forbidding segregation on buses arrived in Montgomery. At five to six on the morning of 21st December – exactly one year and sixteen days after the beginning of the boycott – Martin, his friend Ralph Abernathy and two MIA colleagues boarded a Montgomery bus at the stop outside Martin's home. Press and T.V. were there to record this signal triumph in the cause of civil rights for negroes.

Or rather, it was a triumph on paper. The reality was somewhat different.

It seems incredible that the officials of a city, whether appointed or elected, could deliberately flout a specific direction of the United States' highest court. But it happened. The following announcement was published in

Montgomery:

'The City Commission, and we know our people are with us in this determination, will not yield one inch, but will do all in its power to oppose the integration of the Negro race with the white race in Montgomery, and will forever stand like a rock against social equality, intermarriage, and mixing of the races under God's creation and plan.'

How hypocritical to bring God into this clearly expressed prejudice! What a long way from the words of the Declaration of Independence that 'under God, all men are created equal'!

In any case, the MIA were not asking for intermarriage between black and white. All they were claiming was courteous treatment and a right not to be turned off the buses after paying their fare! The law was on their side but Montgomery had set itself above the law. It would use intimidation if necessary to get its own way.

Buses were once again carrying black passengers but those passengers now were attacked. One coloured woman was shot in the legs; a teenage girl was beaten up. In January, 1957, only a few weeks after the Federal Order had been delivered, four black Baptist churches and the homes of two of their pastors (one of them Ralph Abernathy) were set on fire and completely destroyed. Peace was eventually restored to the city and seven white men were actually arrested and charged with arson and terrorist acts. Needless to say, they were acquitted. No Southern jury would ever find a white man guilty if charged with an offence against a negro.

Martin and his committee had gained a moral victory but it had proved a hollow one. Martin was deeply depressed. On 14th January, 1957, he was addressing a negro rally. He broke off his speech to make the following prayer:

'Lord, I hope no-one will have to die as a result of our struggle for freedom in Montgomery. Certainly, I don't want to die. But if anyone has to die, let it be me.'

He could not have realised how that prayer would be answered.

6. Ambassador at large

By 1957 it was apparent to Martin that the negro was 'in for a season of suffering'. Whatever the legal victories gained by his people, southern obduracy would reduce them to nought. There was a growing call among some sectons of the coloured population for greater militance in the pursuit of their rights but this Martin resisted with every speech he made, every article he wrote.

'Non-violence,' he insisted, '... appeals to the conscience of the great decent majority who through blindness, fear, pride or irrationality have allowed their consciences to sleep.'

As President of the newly formed Southern Negro Leadership Conference (SNLC), Martin invited President Eisenhower or Vice-President Nixon to make a fact-finding tour of the southern states to see for themselves the injustices and insults suffered by negroes. His request was met with polite evasion.

A month later, in February 1957, he again approached the Administration in Washington, this time asking them to hold a conference on civil rights for negroes. Once again, his request met with no success. 'The moment was impropitious' was the official reply.

Despite these setbacks, Martin was convinced that

non-violence was the only right way – indeed, the only Christian way forward. He was confirmed in this view when in March he and Coretta were invited by Dr. Kwame Nkrumah, the first President, to attend the Independence celebrations of the new state of Ghana. In Accra they saw evidence that freedom could be obtained without revolution. The 'Gold Coast' had been subject to British dominion ever since it had been absorbed into the British Empire in 1874 during the reign of Queen Victoria. Now it had become Ghana and there was a peaceful handing over of power. The British Royal Family, represented by H. R. H. Princess Marina, the Duchess of Kent, gave the newly-named state their blessing. Martin was thrilled to see black policemen, black judges, a black President. He was impressed that emancipation could be achieved with peace and friendship and dignity. He was able to dicuss this with Vice-President Nixon who was also in Accra for the celebrations.

That the young civil rights leader had fired the imagination of the world with his courageous and Christian stand was shown by the invitations now showered upon him. He and Coretta returned to Montgomery, but by way of Nigeria, Rome, Geneva, Paris, London and New York. This last call was to discuss the possibility of a mass pilgrimage to Washington which, in fact, took place on 17th May, 1957.

This date was chosen because it was three years to the day since Chief Justice Earl Warren had decreed that segregated education was unfair and illegal. That had been before Martin had been catapulted into the forefront of the civil rights campaign but now, on this Prayer Pilgrimage, he was to be the principal speaker. Well-known negroes like Harry Belafonte, the singer; Sidney Poitier, the actor;

and Sammy Davis, Jnr., the entertainer, addressed the vast crowd – some twenty-five thousand – gathered before the Lincoln Memorial in Washington. But it was Martin they really wanted to hear.

He began with a scathing criticism of the White House's 'silence and apathy' regarding the mounting tumult over race relations. He called upon the Government to ensure that Federal laws were strictly observed, not ignored as in Alabama. He called on the many white citizens of America who believed in Justice and human dignity to be more positive in their support and, equally, he called on black leaders to stress the need among blacks for responsible behaviour. But it was when he reached the question of voting rights that his speech took wings.

Only a small number of negroes throughout the United States were registered as voters, even though, way back in 1773 at the Boston Tea Party which touched off the American War of Independence against Britain, the clarion call had been 'No taxation without representation'. Perhaps that slogan should have read 'No taxation for *whites* without representation'. Now Martin repeated that call on behalf of *black* Americans, five million without the vote in the south alone:

'Give us the ballot,' he insisted.

Give us the ballot and we will no longer have to worry the federal government about our basic rights . . .

We will no longer plead – we will write the proper laws on the books.

Give us the ballot and we will fill the legislature with men of goodwill.

Give us the ballot and we will get the people judges who love mercy.

Give us the ballot and we will quietly, lawfully, and non-violently, without rancour or bitterness, implement the May 17th, 1954 decision of the Supreme

Court.'

As he hammered his point home with the reiterated phrase 'Give us the ballot', there was a rising chorus of 'Amens' and 'Hallelujahs' from the vast crowd assembled to hear him. It was the sort of emotional atmosphere that he had found distasteful in his earlier years but which he found his speeches now evoked.

This address, widely reported throughout America, added greatly to Martin's reputation. His courage and foresight and integrity were rewarded by honorary degrees from Harvard and Chicago universities. He received the Spingarn Medal awarded for work in improving race relations. At twenty-eight, he was the youngest-ever recipient. But all these were personal, superficial successes which were thrust upon him. Far more satisfying was to receive a reply to the letter he had sent to Vice-President Nixon the day before the Prayer Pilgrimage. Now he was invited to meet the Vice-President at the White House on 13th June. Surely something would come of such a meeting!

In the event, Richard Nixon conceded little, though he was gracious at the meeting. However, one outcome was a Civil Rights Bill (albeit a somewhat tame one) passed in September which set up a Commission to look into the question of voting rights for negroes.

Back in Montgomery after the heady events of the past few months, Martin thought deeply about his own position. He reflected on the way he had been fêted in Africa and in Europe, about the distinctions he had been given back in the United States. Those were not going to help the negro in his plight. He thought back to his inspiration, Mahatma Gandhi, and to what he had suffered; he thought of Kwame Nkrumah and his tussles with the British administration. Not for nothing had the women of Montgomery called Martin 'Little Lord Jesus' when his home had been bombed and when he had been arrested in 1956. He realised that, if his leadership was to have any lasting impact, he himself must set an example of physical suffering.

It was a hard decision, particularly as it would affect his wife and baby daughter but Coretta had promised to support him whatever he chose to do. She would not draw back now.

He decided that, if in the future he was charged with any offence, he would accept imprisonment rather than pay an alternative fine. That way he would draw more attention to the negro cause.

The first occasion on which he displayed his new resolve arose out of a simple instance of persecution. On 3rd September, 1957, Ralph Abernathy had to attend court in connection with some private suit – nothing to do with civil rights – and Martin and Coretta, as friends, went with him to give him moral support. Their faces were well-known. Several police, presumably over-reacting to the presence of the civil rights leader and his wife, turned nasty. They swore at the Kings and ordered them to leave the court. Martin protested. They were not breaking any law occupying the public benches. But it seemed that anything he did was an offence in the eyes of the Montgomery police. Martin was seized, his arms twisted up behind his back, and frog-marched off to the police station. There he was charged with 'loitering and failing to obey an officer'.

When his case came before the court a couple of days later, he was fined $10 or fourteen days' imprisonment. True to his resolve, he refused to pay the fine and elected to go to prison instead. It would draw attention to the obvious injustice of the charge against him.

Unfortunately, his white 'opponents' were as quick to recognise their mistake as he was to determine on passive acceptance. Before he had even reached the County gaol, the Police Commissioner, Clyde Sellers, paid his fine for him. 'I'm not going to let him use gaol for his own selfish purposes,' he declared.

Selfish purposes! No negro would enter an American gaol for selfish purposes. Moreover, Commissioner Sellers' action only confirmed in Martin the resolution to use imprisonment as a weapon to illustrate the persecution suffered by his race.

However, he was to be denied any such opportunities for the next few months.

On 20th September, only a couple of weeks after Martin's conviction for 'loitering', he was invited to Blumstein's department store in New York to autograph copies of his newly published first book, 'Stride Toward Freedom', his account of the Montgomery bus boycott. This event in itself illustrates the love/hate relationship the American public had towards the young civil rights leader. One section would haul him before a court on a trumped-up charge – another would queue to obtain his autograph.

On this occasion, it was one of his own people who attacked him. A negro woman, a Mrs. Isola Curry, pushed through the press around him. 'Dr. King?' she asked. Martin looked up with a smile. 'Yes?' he answered – and felt a sudden pain as she rammed an eight inch letter opener up to the hilt into his chest. A press photograph taken at the time shows how incredibly calm Martin remained despite the acute gravity of his position. He said afterwards that he felt God was beside him, giving him support. He was rushed to hospital where surgeons carried out a delicate three-hour operation to remove the paper-knife. 'He was just a sneeze away from death', one of the surgeons reported. The knife had missed his heart by a hairsbreadth. One little girl wrote to him:

'Dear Dr. King,
I'm so glad you didn't sneeze.'

Mrs. Curry, it was found, was quite unbalanced. Her attack bore no relation to Martin's work. She was detained in a mental institution. Martin was concerned that she should receive treatment rather than punishment.

It had been a near thing. After leaving hospital, he was advised to take things very quietly for a time, so he was able to rest and relax with Coretta and the family, gently to pursue his pastoral duties and, for the time being, leave the great and mounting civil rights struggle in other hands.

There was one meeting with President Eisenhower in June, 1958 when Martin and members of his committee begged the President to take a firmer stand on implementing the Supreme Court's rulings against segregation.

'But Reverend,' President Eisenhower had said lamely, 'There are so many problems – Lebanon . . . Algeria . . .'

It seemed that no-one in Washington was prepared to face up to the fact that racism was not one of 'many problems' but was *the* problem for America in the middle of the twentieth century. It was a self-inflicted problem that need never have become so intractable.

Martin could not but compare his own Government's apathy over racism with the Indian Government's active concern regarding the long-entrenched social injustice of the caste system.

He and Coretta went to India in February 1959. They

had been invited the year before by the Gandhi National Memorial Fund but at that time Martin was not sufficiently recovered from the stabbing. Now he felt strong enough to face a lecture tour and to pay his respects to the memory of the man who was such an inspiration to him.

'To other countries I may go as a tourist,' he said on arrival, 'but to India I come as a pilgrim. This is because India means to me Mahatma Gandhi, a truly great man of the age.'

He had a meeting with the Prime Minister, Pandit Nehru (who showed a gratifying familiarity with Martin's work for civil rights). They talked at length about the need to alleviate both racial and religious suffering. This was when Martin learned of Nehru's determination to eradicate the caste system which kept the Indian more firmly trapped in his way of life than even the most vicious segregationist laws kept the negro. Not only had caste discrimination been made punishable by imprisonment; it had been decreed by law that 'untouchables', the lowest caste of all, should be given priority in University admissions. 'This,' Nehru told them, 'is our way of atoning for the centuries of injustice we have inflicted upon these people.'

Wherever their party went, they were received with enthusiasm and attention. Coretta was called upon to sing on many occasions and her lovely rendering of negro spirituals seemed to enthral her Indian audiences. Martin quipped that Coretta sang as much as he lectured!

They travelled to Delhi, Bombay, Calcutta, Madras. They inspected social experiments undertaken by the Indian Government such as the 'untouchable' village set up to provide land for the poorest peasants. They visited the Gandhi Memorial. On 10th March, they returned to the United States, much more informed as to the techniques of non-violence and much more confident of its potency as a weapon against injustice.

Conditions for the negro were as bad as ever when Martin and Coretta returned. There were lynchings of negroes in Mississippi. In Virginia, the School Board of Prince Edward County disbanded its whole education system rather than comply with the laws demanding integration.

There was so much to do. Martin was in demand everywhere – on T.V. in April in a nation-wide programme, 'Meet the Press'; visiting California in May, and Chicago, Detroit, New York and many cities in the south. Early in May, he addressed a luncheon of Trade Union Leaders and the following day, Governor Rockefeller despatched his personal plane to bring Martin to Albany, New York, for a personal discussion on civil rights. How could he travel thus about the United States in pursuit of the negro cause, travel abroad to lecture and enlist international support, yet at the same time remain as pastor of his flock at Dexter Avenue Baptist Church, Montgomery? His church members had been very generous. They had encouraged his work for civil rights. They had not complained when for weeks at a time they were without a pastor. Martin was President of the MIA; President of the SNLC; there was even, as Martin put it, 'the general strain of being known.' He felt strongly that he was not being fair to his church.

So when, in November 1959, his father renewed his invitation to Martin to become co-pastor with him of Ebenezer Baptist Church in Atlanta, Martin knew that the time was right to accept. If he was away on the campaign trail, his father would still be at home to minister to the congregation.

He explained all this in a farewell address to his Montgomery congregation on 29th November, 1959. He had to go on with his work for civil rights.

'I can't stop now,' he said. 'History has thrust something upon me which I cannot turn away.'

7.   Backlash

Early in 1960, there was a groundswell of protest among University students. It came not just from negro students but from white youngsters as well – from a new generation of white Americans not as set in their attitudes as their parents and grandparents. The protest started in February in Greensborough, North Carolina, when a group of black and white students held a 'sit-in' in the local Woolworth store at the lunch counter which was reserved for 'whites only'. They insisted that they would stay on the premises until they were served. Despite abuse from white customers and store employees, they maintained a quiet dignity and stayed until closing time. Soon students in other colleges in North Carolina took a similar attitude. It spread to Atlanta in Georgia and on throughout the southern states to over a hundred cities. Lunch counters, drug stores, restaurants, theatres, swimming-pools, libraries – anywhere where service to negroes was refused – there the students monopolised the seats and refused to move. Sometimes the sit-ins worked; more often, they did not. There were three thousand six hundred arrests.

In the middle of April, the students held a conference at Shaw University in Raleigh, North Carolina. Martin was asked to speak. He called for more co-ordinated planning behind the struggle for civil rights. He called for nationwide action to support businesses that followed non-racial policies and to penalise businesses that did not. Most powerful of all, though, was his call for an army of volunteers who were prepared to suffer, who would go to prison if necessary. He could not have appealed to a more idealistic group of young people than students.

Christ had advocated non-violence as a way of life. Martin called for non-violence to be used as a tactic as well – but only in a spirit of love and reconciliation. 'Our ultimate end must be the creation of the beloved community', he said.

If the students were enthusiastic, a large proportion of Martin's own generation and older negroes were less so. Many of the black community were afraid that Martin was pushing his protest movement too hard and too fast. It might produce a backlash of white reaction. The gains of the nineteen-fifties had been small compared with the size of the problem. Success in law was so often cancelled out by the outright rebellion of whites who defied that law. In fact, the only *real* success was a moral one, in that the whole of the United States – and indeed, the world – was now aware that a Civil Rights struggle was being waged, that negroes had rights that were being denied them.

Martin himself was constantly harassed. In May 1960 he received an emergency call to visit a patient in the Emory University Hospital. This was just over the border from Atlanta in De Kalb County. In his hurry to reach the hospital, he forgot that his licence to drive into another state had expired so, when he was stopped, he had to admit to the offence. Normally, a driver with an otherwise clean licence who had the excuse of being called out to see a sick member of his church would have been treated leniently. But because he was Martin Luther King, regarded by white police as a black agitator, he was taken to court and placed on probation for twelve months – quite a stiff penalty for a first offence – and fined as well.

More distressing for Martin was an accusation that he had submitted perjured tax returns. To have to stand trial on such a charge was the most serious thing that had happened to him – far worse for a man of his integrity to have the finger of suspicion pointed at him than to have his house bombed. He had never had any interest in amassing a personal fortune. All the prizes and awards he had received for his civil rights work had been devoted to the cause and had been properly accounted for. And he *had* made an honest tax declaration. Yet he had to endure weeks of adverse publicity in the weeks leading up to the trial. Newspapers revelled in the scandal. At the trial, it emerged that the false accusations against him had been laid by someone determined to wreck his work. Martin was acquitted – and by a *white* jury – but the humiliation of that particular court appearance sorely wounded him. As he said, he had been 'bombed, jailed and shot at' but, notwithstanding his acquittal, the tax case caused him the most pain because it was a slur on his reputation.

At least the publicity surrounding the case caused the great Mrs. Eleanor Roosevelt, widow of President Franklin D. Roosevelt, to make a public declaration of her support for him.

1960 was Election Year in the United States so Martin wrote to both the Republican and the Democratic parties asking if they would be prepared to hear him regarding matters he would like them to include in their respective manifestos.

The Republicans did not bother to reply. The Democratic party showed more interest. Its two candidates, Senators John F. Kennedy and Hubert Humphrey, agreed to address a meeting of civil rights leaders in July in Los Angeles. Of the two, Hubert

Humphrey had the better reception. He said that he 'would rather be right about civil rights than be President or Vice-President'. John F. Kennedy's speech was interrupted by boos from the audience. It was Martin who received the rapturous ovation. 'We want to be free everywhere,' he cried. 'Free at last! Free at last!'

It would have been prudent for the leaders of the nation to listen to Martin for his was not the only voice lifted on behalf of the under-privileged negro. Malcolm X and his Black Muslims were a growing menace. They sought to join forces with Martin and his organisation but were totally rejected. Their policy spelled race hatred and violence. The gulf between Martin and Malcolm X was unbridgeable. Martin advocated passive resistance, non-violence and love. Malcolm X believed more could be gained through revolution, violence and hatred.

Martin could have been excused if his own sense of love and forgiveness had occasionally wavered for certainly there was a deal of hatred directed towards him personally.

On October 19th, 1960, Martin supported a student sit-in in Atlanta. Thirty-six youngsters demanded to be served at Rich's department store. As usual, they were refused service. As usual, they stayed where they were. As usual, the police were called and they were all arrested. But whereas the students were fined and sent home, Martin had to suffer the indignity of being taken in handcuffs, like a common criminal, from the Atlanta County Gaol to De Kalb County Gaol to face an additional charge of 'being in breach of his twelve months' probation order' for the motoring offence. It is doubtful whether it is right in law to count an offence in one state to be a breach of a probation order in another but, even if it were, the penalty imposed was savage. Judge Oscar Mitchell sentenced Martin to four months' hard labour in a rural penal camp!

When news of this appeared in the press, telegrams from all over the world arrived at the White House protesting at this cruel treatment of Dr. Martin Luther King. No-one had any doubt that the unwarrantably harsh sentence was part of the 'white backlash' that had been feared.

The White House was nervous. President Eisenhower, its Republican incumbent, was running for a second term of office. The Presidential elections were only weeks away. What would be the effect on the largely white Republican vote if he were seen to intervene on behalf of a negro? He decided to do nothing.

John F. Kennedy was equally perplexed as to the effect there would be on *his* chances for President if *he* intervened. Neither side seemed prepared to judge the case on its merits but only on the grounds of political expediency. In the event, John Kennedy decided to take a chance – a small chance. He phoned through to Coretta to express his sympathy while his lawyer brother, Robert, brought pressure to bear on Judge Mitchell to release Martin on bail pending an appeal.

Daddy King was so relieved that, although he had been a staunch Republican all his life, he told his congregation that he was going to vote this time for the Democratic candidate, John F. Kennedy.

'It took courage,' he said in his Sunday sermon, 'to call my daughter-in-law at a time like this. Kennedy has the moral courage to stand up for what he knows is right.'

A number of negroes who had the vote probably changed their allegiance following this incident. Senator Kennedy was elected President by a very slender majority and it was generally believed that the small but important negro vote swung the election.

Martin was grateful to be freed from 'hard labour' but was shrewd enough to realise that it was merely a political gesture that had won his freedom. In an article in *The Nation* he called on the new Kennedy administration to live up to its progressive slogans and to take a new, more positive approach to civil rights.

Alas for his hopes!

Judges in America are political appointments. The first three southern judges appointed by the Kennedy administration were all avowed segregationists!

8. Freedom Rides

As Martin's message of non-violent protest spread across the United States, so other groups than his own began to take action. In May 1961 there began the 'Freedom Rides' directed against segregation on buses and railways. Their purpose was to test whether the Federal law against segregation was being obeyed and to attract public attention if it was not.

Seven negroes and six white sympathisers boarded the long-distance inter-State bus in Washington and claimed the right to be taken to Birmingham, Alabama, a southern centre of strong anti-negro feeling. When the bus reached Anniston, Alabama, it was attacked and set on fire. The Freedom Riders were scared off but a party of students bravely volunteered to continue the Ride on another bus. *They* were attacked and beaten up when they reached Birmingham.

Yet another group set out for Montgomery. At each stop, ugly mobs of whites formed threatening reception committees. The local police either could not or would not protect the Freedom Riders.

President Kennedy was concerned at the growing level of violence. When the Freedom Riders reached Montgomery, he sent seven hundred Federal Marshals to protect them (that is, national police as opposed to local or state police).

Martin had gone to Montgomery to support the Freedom Riders who, with him, were virtually under siege in Ralph Abernathy's church. If the Federal Marshals had not been present, the angry lynch-mob outside could well have broken in. Martin expressed his gratitude for the protection they were receiving.

'The law may not be able to make a man love me,' he said, 'but it can keep him from lynching me. Freedom Riders must develop the quiet courage of dying for a cause. We would not like to see anyone die . . . but we are well aware that we may have some casualties.'

Meantime, Governor John Patterson declared martial law and, in a panic, phoned Robert Kennedy, the President's brother and Attorney-General, to say he could not guarantee Martin's safety. However, the following morning, protected by six armed soldiers on the bus, with armed National Guards on both sides of the street, with two battalions of the National Guard as escort, with twenty-two highway patrol cars, with three Army reconnaissance planes and two Army helicopters circling overhead, and with seventeen newspaper reporters in attendance, the bus carrying twelve Freedom Riders left Montgomery for Jackson, Mississippi, further and deeper into the South.

It was gratifying that central government was showing so much concern but Martin was appalled that all this display of strength was necessary to guarantee twelve American citizens their right to ride on a bus.

Robert Kennedy now called for a 'cooling off period' but one of the Freedom Riders' leaders retorted 'We've been cooling off for a hundred years. If we get any cooler, we'll be in a deep freeze.' So, throughout the summer, Freedom Riders poured into the Deep South and hundreds were arrested.

Albany, Georgia, was the next place that flared into open protest. This time the demands were not just for integrated lunch counters and restaurants. The target was for recognition of the negro community by the appointment of black policemen and so forth. Dr. Anderson, leader of the black community in Albany, phoned Martin and asked for his support. On 16th December 1961, Martin again used his skill as an orator to restore the flagging spirits of the protestors. 'Don't stop now. Don't get weary, children,' was his message.

The marches and demonstrations went on throughout the spring and summer of 1962. Thousands were arrested. Martin was put in prison three times, refusing to pay fines 'for disorderly conduct and parading without a permit'. But the authorities were getting wise to the national sympathy his imprisonments attracted. On one occasion the judge 'suspended' his sentence – that is, he would not have to serve it unless he was convicted for another offence. His fines were paid for him, despite his protests, and he was, to use his own phrase, 'thrown out of prison'.

In May, Martin wrote to President Kennedy describing conditions in Albany and begging him to use his influence to improve the conditions of negro housing, education, employment and the like. But the President, conscious of his slender majority, vacillated . . . did nothing.

Still pursuing their ends by peaceful means, Martin, Ralph and Dr. Anderson and ten other negroes knelt on the pavement outside the Albany city hall on 27th July and prayed that God would open the eyes and soften the hearts of the city officials within. There were no crowds, no singing, no shouting – but they were all arrested, just the same.

Others followed their example, day after day, with quiet but public prayer. By the end of the week, over one thousand negroes had been put in gaol.

The foreign press looked on with amazement and scorn. How, they wondered in their articles, could America square its talk of democracy with the barbarous reality of its treatment of blacks? President Kennedy still seemed nervous to take any firm action. He went so far as to 'deplore' in a public statement the refusal of the Albany city officials to confer with the black leaders, but that was all. It was not enough, and Martin said so in a scathing article in the New York Times.

There was, nonetheless, growing white support for the negro cause. Seventy-five white ministers and rabbis joined in the demonstrations in Albany and in prayers on the pavement outside the court-house. They supported the efforts of the negroes to worship in hitherto segregated churches; they supported their efforts to obtain service in restaurants. But, alas, no sooner had this white demonstration of solidarity finished and the ministers and rabbis left for their own homes, than the Ku Klux Klan swung into action. There was a brief and intimidating period of terror when negro churches were bombed and burnt. This time, there was no seeming 'miracle' of a Supreme Court ruling as there had been in Montgomery to buoy up the courage of the negroes. Here in Albany the Ku Klux Klan was able to rampage unhindered.

When it was over, life in Albany reverted to 'normal' – with the condition of the negro population worse than before their protests. By the end of 1962, not only were there no black policemen in Albany. Negroes were forbidden to use the public parks or the public swimming pools or the public libraries.

Albany, as a civil rights demonstration, had been a dismal failure.

9.   Confrontation

After the Albany débacle, Martin felt near despair. It seemed that for every step forward he made over civil rights, he slipped back two. Of course, he was fighting against three hundred and fifty years of prejudice. There were still some negroes alive who had been born into slavery as, indeed, had been his own grandfather on his father's side. He decided that the only way forward would be to have a civil rights success on such a scale that the Federal Government would not be able to ignore it. Not a *victory* – that would only cause resentment in the vanquished. He wanted a success that would bring such enormous publicity that the Government would have to bring in the last remaining pieces of legislation necessary to give the negroes their full rights and, then, to implement those laws.

What would be the best target?

Birmingham, the capital of Alabama, had in Eugene 'Bull' Connor a Police Chief with a reputation for cruelty over law enforcement. Blacks in Birmingham lived in terror of police brutality. It would take enormous physical and moral courage to oppose *him* but a victory in Birmingham would be a victory indeed.

Early in January, 1963, Martin went to Birmingham to plan the campaign with the local leaders. He felt that the failure of Albany had been in part due to haphazard

69

planning.

First of all, he set out to train his fellow blacks in the techniques of non-violence. Martin's strength lay in his insistence on Christian principles being observed by all demonstrators. Love must be shown at all costs.

'Love your enemies,' Jesus had insisted. 'Do good to those who hate you; bless those who curse you; pray for those who treat you spitefully.' (Luke 6.27)

To this end, every demonstrator in the Birmingham campaign was asked to sign a Commitment Card, promising as follows:

'I hereby pledge myself – my person and body – to the non-violent movement. Therefore, I will keep the following Ten Commandments:

1. *Meditate* daily on the teachings and life of Jesus.
2. *Remember* always that the non-violent movement in Birmingham seeks justice and reconciliation, not victory.
3. *Walk and Talk* in the manner of love, for God is love.
4. *Pray* daily to be used by God in order that all men might be free.
5. *Sacrifice* personal wishes in order that all men might be free.
6. *Observe* with both friend and foe the ordinary rules of courtesy.
7. *Seek* to perform regular service for others and for the world.
8. *Refrain* from the violence of fist, tongue or heart.
9. *Strive* to be in good spiritual and bodily health.
10. *Follow* the directions of the movement and of the captain on a demonstration.

I sign this pledge, having seriously considered what I do
and with the determination and will to persevere.

............(Signature)

Then Martin went on a whirlwind speaking tour
throughout the Southern states to raise funds for the
Birmingham campaign. Funds were necessary for various
reasons: to support the families of those imprisoned; to
provide back-up services for demonstrators (food, first aid
and so on); to cover the costs of circulars, notices, placards
and the like; and, most of all, to pay the fines of those
imprisoned or to put up money for bail. In England, bail is
granted on the *promise* that money will be paid over if the
conditions of bail are broken. In the United States,
however, the bail money has in practise to be deposited in
cash with the court before a prisoner can be released.

The campaign began on April 3rd, 1963 with a
'Birmingham Manifesto' setting out the grievances of the
black community. Each day there were protest marches
and prayer sessions; each evening there was a public
meeting to boost morale. At first, the response of the
Birmingham police was a mild one but on 10th April,
Judge W. A. Jenkins issued an injunction against every
conceivable type of protest, whether it be a march, a
boycott, a sit-in or whatever. The injunction specifically
named Martin, Ralph and one or two of the other leaders.

Martin felt strongly that the authorities, in taking out
such a comprehensive injunction, were twisting the law
for their own ends and that such an injunction was
therefore unjust. He also felt that the various laws on
segregation that were in force in Birmingham were also
unjust in that they degraded the negro. Thus, for the first
time, he faced up to the problem which Gandhi had had
repeatedly to face: should he obey an unjust law?

71

Jesus had said 'Pay Caesar what is due to Caesar' (Mark 12.17) which implied that one should obey the civil law. Equally cogent, however, was Peter's reply to the doctors of the law in Jerusalem when he asked 'Is it right in God's eyes for us to obey you rather than God?' (Acts 4.19). Martin decided on this occasion that, like Gandhi, he would disobey an unjust law but that, again like Gandhi, he would willingly accept the penalty for such disobedience.

On Good Friday, 12th April, after spending the previous twenty-four hours in fasting and in soul-searching prayer that his decision was right and not in any way tainted by a desire for self-seeking publicity, Martin, with Ralph and fifty volunteers, walked quietly towards the City Hall in defiance of the injunction. In their way stood 'Bull' Connor and his array of police. Martin's group continued forward, without a voice being raised in anger, without a threatening gesture being made. Fifty-two men, quietly determined.

They were all arrested. No-one made any resistance as they were hustled away to the local gaol.

Martin was placed in solitary confinement. He was refused access to a telephone; he was not allowed to call his lawyer. This was bad enough but, because all the funds raised were banked in Martin's name and no-one was allowed to see him, it was impossible for his supporters outside to lay hands on any cash to put down as bail money for the release of the fifty-one detained along with him.

Good Friday moved into Saturday. Still there was utter silence about Martin's whereabouts. Easter Sunday came and there was again no word of him. Meantime, Ralph and the fifty other demonstrators had to stay behind bars.

First thing on Easter Monday, 15th April, news came that Harry Belafonte, the negro singer, had managed over the weekend to raise $50,000 to use as bail money. At least the fifty-one demonstrators could be released pending trial. But what of Martin? Newspapers had begun asking questions. Where was he? Was he still alive? Had he been murdered? Such things were known to happen. One negro's life was not held at any great value in the United States.

Coretta was beside herself with worry. In desperation, she phoned the White House and asked to speak to President Kennedy. He was not available, she was told, but they would pass a message to him. She waited, tense, anxious. Outside, the streets were wrapped in holiday quiet. At last, the sound of the telephone bell broke the stillness. Dexter, their two-year-old third child, grabbed the telephone and chattered into the mouthpiece. Coretta seized the handset from him and heard the White House operator impatiently asking the child to get off the line as the President of the United States wanted to speak to his mother! With beating heart, Coretta waited for President Kennedy to come to the phone. He expressed his concern and sympathy and assured Coretta that he would have enquiries made. Some time later, to her intense relief, Martin came through to his wife on the telephone. The President had insisted that Martin be allowed to speak to his wife. He was safe and well but still in custody.

During his period in solitary confinement, Martin set down his thoughts on the civil rights struggle in his 'Letter from Birmingham Jail'. At first he had to scribble on the margins of newspapers as he had no writing paper but then a black 'trusty' smuggled in some scraps of paper which made writing easier. When (thanks to the President's intervention) Martin at last saw his lawyer, he was able to obtain a proper writing pad. The 'Letter' was completed in four days. Why, it asked, was he, a citizen of Atlanta, in

Birmingham?

'. . . I am in Birmingham,' he wrote, 'because injustice is here . . . Just as the Apostle Paul left his little village of Tarsus and carried the gospel of Jesus Christ to practically every hamlet and city of the Graeco-Roman world, I, too, am compelled to carry the gospel of freedom beyond my particular home town . . .'

Perhaps the intervention of the President on the side of the negroes was having some small effect. On 20th April, Martin was released on bail and, when his trial came up six days later, he was only fined.

Back in circulation again, Martin and Ralph continued with the campaign. It took a great deal of soul-searching to put the next phase of the overall plan into action – to agree to let children march. But the children wanted to. It was their future at stake. On 2nd May, six thousand children, aged from six to sixteen, marched into the city, wave upon wave of them, singing and chanting 'Freedom!' Connor's men were waiting. Nine hundred and fifty-nine children were arrested and that number would have been greater had there been more buses available to take the 'prisoners' away.

That did not stop the children. The next day, they were out again, praying and singing. This time the police showed real brutality. They set snarling dogs onto the marching youngsters, laid about with their night-sticks (truncheons) and turned high-pressure waterhoses onto the children. Newspaper photographs of an alsatian dog with a child's arm in its jaws appalled readers the length and breadth of the United States.

Martin was strongly criticised for allowing children to march but he retorted that there had been no concern 'when down through the years, Negro infants were born into ghettos.'

The next three days were more violent still. Connor had two thousand negroes in prison but still thousands more were prepared to march and to suffer beatings and imprisonment for the cause in which they believed. At times, even the police were sickened by the violence. On 5th May, one of the local Baptist ministers was confronted on a march by the usual line of police. 'Turn on your water, turn loose your dogs,' cried the minister. 'We will stay here till we die!'

Nothing happened.

'Dammit, turn on your hoses!' shouted Connor to his men. But they found they could not. The marchers moved quietly through the police lines; said prayers of thanks for their deliverance; and as quietly dispersed.

In an attempt to bring the violence to an end, Martin had a meeting with Mayor-Elect Boutwell. He presented the terms of the demonstrators. They were the usual modest requests but, again as usual, all were refused.

Police violence against demonstrators increased. As the hours wore on, Connor's men tried to drive the blacks back to their own section of the city. Under their brutal attack, discipline broke down and some negroes retaliated with stones and bottles. The black church leaders tried desperately to restore order.

On Tuesday, 7th May, Martin had another meeting with the white authorities. This time, a hundred and twenty-five leaders of the Birmingham Chamber of Commerce were present. The talk swung backwards and forwards, Martin pressing for a less violently racist atmosphere in Birmingham; the whites remaining as intransigent as ever. Then, above the weary arguments in the Council Chamber, there rose the sound of singing – a mounting, swelling surge of voices as thousands of negroes converged on the building, singing their 'battle hymn': 'We Shall Overcome'. It was awe-inspiring. When the members of the meeting looked out through the windows of the Council Chamber, they saw a sea of upturned black faces. There were negroes everywhere, thousands of them, standing and sitting on the pavements, blocking the roads, cramming the shop doorways.

White resistance began to weaken – though not to give way entirely. Eventually, a truce was called. The white leaders would further consider the negroes' requests if Martin would call off his demonstrations. This he agreed to do – with the warning that the marches would start again on Thursday if there was no progress towards an agreement.

But a truce meant nothing to 'Bull' Connor.

Immediately, and for no reason, he arrested Martin and Ralph and put them in prison again. Black anger flared. The arrest was an outrageous breach of the truce. Another march was called for and Birmingham looked all set for a season of bloodshed.

This time the Federal authorities could not just look on. Robert Kennedy intervened, appealing to the negroes to cancel their march and promising to get the two leaders freed. Martin and Ralph were released on bail and on the following day, Thursday, May 9th, the negotiators on the side of the whites agreed to all the conditions proposed by Martin, except for the one asking for charges against those arrested to be dropped.

There was one more surge of extreme violence when Martin's brother's home in Birmingham was bombed and also the headquarters of the campaign at the Gaston Motel. Then the attacks on the negroes stopped. The marches and demonstrations came to an uneasy end.

Martin had had the 'success' he was looking for.

On 11th June, 1963, President Kennedy at last

announced that he was asking Congress to enact immediately the most comprehensive Civil Rights Bill to date.

'One hundred years of delay have passed,' he said in an Address to the Nation, 'since President Lincoln freed the slaves, yet their heirs, their grandsons, are not fully free . . . And this nation, for all its hopes and all its boasts, will not be fully free until all its citizens are free.

We preach freedom around the world, and we mean it, and we cherish our freedom here at home, but are we to say to the world . . . that this is a land of the free except for the Negroes . . .?

The events in Birmingham and elsewhere have so increased the cries for equality that no city or state or legislative body can prudently choose to ignore them . . .'.

It was eight years since Martin had taken the lead in civil rights affairs and, at last, he had made his mark on Washington.

10. 'I have a dream...'

Martin was by now a national and international figure, the undisputed and widely respected head of the Civil Rights movement. There were worrying outbreaks of violence from black militants which only served to highlight the Christian example set by Martin with his plea for love and only peaceful protest.

After Birmingham, he went on what can only be called a 'triumphant tour' across America, from California on the west coast to New York on the east. In Chicago, he addressed a crowd of ten thousand. In Detroit on June 23rd he led a hundred and twenty-five thousand people on a 'Freedom Walk' down Woodward Avenue. In his speech on this occasion he spoke words which men would remember and quote to each other only a few years later:

'... If a man hasn't discovered something he will die for, he isn't fit to live,' Martin said, urging his hearers to put their all into the civil rights campaign.

He did not spare himself and he looked to his followers to give the same dedication. More and more, his noble example was winning white support to his campaign and when 'Birmingham-type' protests erupted in other parts of America that summer, they were supported by white Americans as well as black.

Of course, the way of love is slow to show results. It has taken two thousand years for Christianity to spread

79

through the world and its message is still not understood. Little wonder that Martin's campaign of peaceful protest brought an impatient reaction from those blacks who rejected his Christian approach. They hurled rotten eggs at his car in New York.

President Kennedy's Civil Rights Bill was not having the easy progress through Congress that he had hoped for. In fact, it was threatened by the filibustering tactics of the Opposition – that is, deliberately putting obstructions in the way of getting a law passed, like making speeches that went on for hours, holding up business.

Martin felt it was time to implement the Washington March which he and his leaders had been planning for some months. It was not to be an intimidating march but rather an effort at 'creative lobbying' and, as the March would be in Washington at the very seat of government, it would remind Congress of the need for the Civil Rights Bill to become law as soon as possible.

At first, President Kennedy was doubtful about the march. He feared it might lead to civil disorder in the capital but this fear was eased when he found that some members of the government were prepared to co-operate; also, business people and the negro leaders. All wanted to make the march a success. Two thousand black members of the New York police force volunteered to come to Washington to act as marshals.

The event would take the form of a peaceful march down Pennsylvania Avenue to the Lincoln Memorial where there would be an entertainment and speeches. Before the march began, its leaders would explain their case to members of Congress. After the march, those same leaders would meet President Kennedy. It was expected that a hundred and fifty thousand people would take part but, on the day, 28th August 1963, some quarter of a million people thronged the broad processional avenue. It was estimated that about half of these were white.

It was a happy occasion in the hot summer sun. Bob Dylan, Sammy Davis, Jnr., Lena Horne and Harry Belafonte entertained the crowds. Joan Baez sang 'We Shall Overcome' and thousands of voices responded with 'Amen! Amen!' The group, Peter, Paul and Mary, sang 'How many times must a man look up, Before he can reach the sky . . .' The crowd were ecstatic. Speeches were deliberately kept low-key. This was a demonstration, not a revolution. But the man the great throng were waiting to hear was Martin Luther King.

He took his stand on the podium with the vast statue of President Lincoln rising up behind him – that statue to which all American children are taken when in Washington, as representing the man who established all that is best in the American way of life.

'Five score years ago,' Martin began, 'a great American, in whose symbolic shadow we stand, signed the Emancipation Proclamation. But one hundred years later we must face the tragic fact that the Negro is still not free.

One hundred years later, the life of the Negro is still sadly crippled by the manacles of segregation and the chains of discrimination.

One hundred years later, the Negro lives on a lonely island of poverty in the midst of a vast ocean of material prosperity . . .'

The rich, musical voice gathered strength to a rising tide of 'Amens' and 'Alleluias' from the listening crowds. The slanting almond-shaped eyes became visionary as Martin launched into his peroration:

'I have a dream that one day this nation will rise up, live out the true meaning of its creed . . .

I have a dream that the children of slaves and slave-owners will one day live in brotherhood...

I have a dream that one day my children will be judged not by their colour but by their character...

This will be the day when all God's children, black man and white man, Jews and Gentiles, Protestants and Catholics, will be able to join hands and sing in the words of the old Negro spiritual, "Free at last! Free at last! Great God Almighty, we are free at last!" '

This was more than a speech about the black/white civil rights struggle. Martin wanted, with all the passion of the dedicated Christian, to rid the world of the hatred and fear and prejudice and ignorance that have led to the tragedies of the Middle East, of Northern Ireland, of South Africa, of Poland... Wherever in the world there was intolerance and a clash of ideologies, he wanted the light of Christ's love to enter in.

But in the meantime, he and his colleagues had to attend their promised meeting with President Kennedy, Vice-President Lyndon B. Johnson and the Secretary for Labour. It was no surprise to the negro leaders to find the President, as usual, lacking in decision over the civil rights issue, despite the brave words of his Address to the Nation on 11th June. He was not at all sure, he said, of getting through the section of his Bill relating to Equal Employment opportunities and suggested that the black leaders drop their insistence on this clause and settle for what they could get.

However, it was just this point of being able to get jobs on equal terms with whites that was so important. If a negro could not earn as good money as a white, how could he ever enjoy the good home and good school that white Americans enjoyed – all the things that would raise him up from the depressed condition in which he lived and worked?

So the black leaders refused to trim their demands. They insisted that the President keep all the clauses in the Bill and that he should try to get the Bill through Congress in its entirety.

Inevitably, there was a white backlash. On 15th September, a black church in Birmingham was dynamited. Twenty-one negroes were injured and four little girls were killed. There was outrage among the black community. In the ensuing turmoil, the police shot and killed two black teenagers. Was the Birmingham 'success' to be no more than an illusion?

Even with these setbacks, the momentum of the civil rights movement was increasing all over the country. Martin had high hopes that the President, sensing this change of mood, might be transformed from a hesitant leader into a much stronger and more resolute one. That, surely, would be the outcome if he won the 1964 Presidential Election and returned to the White House for a second term of office.

It was not to be.

On 22nd November, 1963, two bullets fired from a high-velocity rifle through an upper window of the Texas Book depository Building in Dallas, Texas, put an end to the Presidency of John F. Kennedy. His assassination shocked a world whose imagination had been captured by the youth and debonair good looks of the President, rather than by his achievements.

Martin himself was appalled. Although he had protested vigorously about the President's slowness to act over civil rights, he had nonetheless enjoyed good relations with him, and he would always be grateful for the concern he and his brother, Robert, had shown over

Martin's various periods of imprisonment. Martin was, in fact, one of the twelve hundred mourners invited to the funeral service in St. Matthew's Cathedral, Washington – this in itself a singular and noticeable demonstration of respect for a negro.

Debate still continues as to who really killed President Kennedy and why. Martin was more gravely concerned over the 'how' and the 'what' of the assassination. He wrote bitterly condemning America's 'morally inclement climate . . . a climate where men cannot disagree without being disagreeable, and where they express their disagreement through violence and murder . . .'

Was there to be no end to the killings, to the beatings-up, to the lynchings and the bombings? Had America made no progress at all since the violence of its frontier days or the cold-blooded cruelty of its gangster wars?

He was deeply depressed and so were his colleagues in the negro struggle. President Kennedy had been hesitant but he had at least set in motion a new Civil Rights Bill. He had been succeeded in office by his Texan Vice-President, Lyndon B. Johnson. What possible hope could there be for negroes under a President from the Deep South?

On 26th November, four days after the assassination, the various Civil Rights leaders held a meeting and, in a collective press statement, called for the immediate passage of the Civil Rights legislation as a tribute to the late President. Amazingly, on the following day, the new President asked Congress to end the deadlock over the Bill and to submit a strong civil rights package for his approval!

A week later, on 3rd December 1963, Martin had a fifty minute interview with President Johnson. He had already met him at the meeting after the Washington March but now he was the most powerful man in the United States rather than just the deputy. It was an indication of how important he considered the negro problem to be that he should elect to meet Martin so soon after taking office in such confused and tragic circumstances. In the event, the Civil Rights Bill became law some months later, on 2nd July, 1964.

A further indication of Martin's growing stature on the national scene came on 3rd January, 1964 when his face appeared on the cover of the prestigious *Time* Magazine by which he had been chosen 'Man of the Year'. He was only the second black to be so chosen – the other had been Emperor Haile Selassie of Ethiopia in 1927.

Time, in its tribute to Martin, wrote:

'By deed and by preachment, he has stirred in his people a Christian forebearance that nourishes hope and smothers injustice.'

1964 was going to be another year for 'smothering injustice'. This time, Martin's target was to ensure the Southern negro's right to vote.

11.   Valleys and Mountains

Although negroes represented approximately one tenth of the population of the United States, relatively few of them enjoyed the right to vote, even in 1964. Although technically, they *possessed* the right, very few of them were able to exercise it because, before being able to vote, it was necessary to register as a voter. Even today, a million negroes remain unregistered but in 1964 registration had been neglected because negroes did not know of their rights, or, through lack of education, did not know how to claim them. Some could not even read or write which, at that time, would automatically disqualify them from being allowed to register. When the steady campaign of men such as Martin made them aware of their rights, negroes found that, in some areas, they were actively prevented from registering. Not only was there positive intimidation but also more subtle methods were used.

A negro would arrive at his Town Hall to register, only to be told 'We've finished registrations for this month. Come back in four weeks' time.' Or there would be a queue waiting to register. A couple of names would be taken, then the counter would be closed. 'That's all we're doing for today.'

In March 1964, Martin asked that Federal Marshals be sent to the South to guarantee the right of negroes to register without intimidation. He himself went to St.

Augustine in Florida where constant attacks by the Ku Klux Klan were causing panic among the black community. The new Governor of Florida, Haydon Burns, was a rabid segregationalist who did nothing to stop the reign of terror.

Martin organised marches to support those wishing to place their names on the voting register. Rowdies attacked them with chains and clubs. Then the local Sheriff forbade any marches after 6.30 p.m. Martin countered by instructing his lawyers to obtain a Federal injunction against the Sheriff and by 9th June, evening meetings were declared legal.

Nevertheless, that night, police and white vigilantes attacked and broke up a meeting that Martin was to address. He was arrested – yet again.

The manager of the local swimming pool in St. Augustine poured sulphuric acid into the water, rather than allow any negroes to enjoy the use of it. To such extremes did white prejudice extend!

However, as mentioned already, President Johnson's Civil Rights Bill became law on 2nd July. It was comprehensive in its terms and St. Augustine went some way towards obeying it. Indeed, the same applied to some other areas and for the first time for months, the black/white confrontation seemed to be less impassioned.

But only *seemed*.

Whereas Martin's civil rights campaign consisted of peaceful demonstrations organised largely by black clergy, the Black Power Movement was encouraged by its leaders to use violence to achieve its aims. The oppressive heat of New York in late July would always give rise to tension in the slum areas of Harlem and this year of 1964 needed little encouragement from agitators to start riots among the blacks in the district. When the violence seemed to be getting beyond police control, Mayor Wagner sent an urgent message to Martin, begging him to use his influence to quell the troubles.

Martin flew immediately to New York – and to another disastrous failure.

He had, in his anxiety to help, made two fundamental mistakes: he had not consulted his fellow black leaders, which gave rise to criticism that he was becoming self-important; even worse, he had not consulted the leaders of the Harlem community as to whether they wanted him there. Those who did not like his non-violent message misrepresented his visit: what did a southern preacher know of New York's problems? Martin realised all too soon the mistakes he had made and the futility of his visit. There was nothing for it but to return to the south.

It was not a good summer for the movement.

Despite the Civil Rights Act, there was violence in the air. More rioting broke out in the north, while much more sinister things were happening in the south.

Many white university students had been greatly moved by the Washington March the previous summer, with its emphasis on the brotherhood of man. Now, in the long summer vacation of 1964, many of them went south to Mississippi to talk, to teach, to try to bring to fruition the ideals expressed in Martin's 'I have a dream' speech. Alas, a number of these young white idealists just disappeared, presumably murdered for daring to speak against the southern tradition of rigidly enforced segregation.

1964 was in addition Election Year for a new President. Election fever swept the country, exacerbating any unrest that already existed. President Johnson was the Democratic candidate, seeking re-election after his year in office following the assassination of President Kennedy. His opponent in the Presidential race was Senator Barry

Goldwater, a Republican candidate of extreme views. Martin and some of the civil rights leaders were concerned that an upsurge of black lawlessness would cause the largely white electorate to react against the negroes and vote for Goldwater. Thus they advised that there should be a halt to demonstrations until after the election – though not everyone agreed with them.

Martin went on TV to say that he was proposing to put up to the Democratic Convention a 'Bill of Rights for the Disadvantaged'. He realised that the phase of demanding service at the lunch counter in a Woolworth store was over; the time was ripe to attack the greater evils of poverty and bad housing. Until the negro could face life on equal terms with whites – be able to earn as much, learn as much, live as well – he would always stay a second-class citizen. Moreover, bad conditions gave rise to sloth and apathy. Martin always stressed the importance of 'racial worthiness'. Just as, from being a schoolboy, he had sought to prevent the epithet 'dirty nigger' being applied to him, so he urged every negro to do his best at all times. 'If you are a street sweeper,' he said, 'you ought to be the best possible.' St. Paul had said 'Whatever you are doing, put your whole heart into it, as if you were doing it for the Lord and not for men.' (Col. 3.23).

To help the negro out of the pit of sloth and apathy, he advocated at the Democratic Convention in Atlantic City a Bill to provide money to lift negroes out of poverty. President Johnson's administration voted one billion dollars for this purpose – less than Martin had hoped for but a step in the right direction. This, together with the Civil Rights Act, were two positive actions by President Johnson's Democratic administration.

Indications of the growing respect abroad for Martin's work came with invitations for him to visit Amsterdam in

September, followed by visits to West and East Berlin, to Madrid and to Rome where he was received in audience by Pope Paul VI. The crowning reward came in October when it was announced that he had been awarded the Nobel Peace Prize for 1964. At thirty-five, he was the youngest person ever to receive the award; and he was only the third negro, the others being Dr. Ralph Bunche and Chief Albert Luthuli.

American reaction to the news of the award varied from enormous and natural pride on the part of Daddy King; rejoicing by the negro community that their struggle for equal rights had now received international recognition; and disgust on the part of southern whites. Typical was 'Bull' Connor's remark: 'Shame on somebody!'

On 6th December, Martin, along with Coretta, his parents and Ralph Abernathy, flew to London. Martin made two public speeches: at the City Temple he denounced South Africa's policy of *apartheid*; at St. Paul's Cathedral – the first non-Anglican to preach there in the Cathedral's two hundred and ninety one year history – he gave a moving sermon on 'The Three Dimensions of the Complete Life'.

Then it was on to Norway and all the pageantry of the Nobel Prize ceremony. The Reverend Ake Zetterburg of Stockholm said of him 'He has proved that he can take setbacks without losing courage or abandoning his ideals. His unarmed struggle is a model case . . .'.

Martin himself, with true humility, accepted the prize as a tribute to all those unnamed negroes who had worked and suffered with him in the civil rights movement that was still 'beleaguered'. He pointed out that they had not yet won 'the very peace and brotherhood which is the essence of the Nobel Prize.' He concluded that the award was a recognition that 'non-violence is the answer to . . .

the need for man to overcome oppression and violence without resorting to violence and oppression.' He continued: '. . . I have the audacity to believe that peoples everywhere can have three meals a day for their bodies, education and culture for their minds, and dignity, equality and freedom for their spirits . . .' All this would be achieved because his fellow negroes (and, indeed, other oppressed peoples) – 'these humble children of God', he called them – were willing to suffer for righteousness' sake.

This was the Martin Luther King of international stature, looking wider than the campaign for civil rights for negroes in the United States. He was making an appeal for the rights of all oppressed minorities, of all the poor and hungry in the world. If only mankind could seek to solve its problems through love rather than violence, there could be hope for all these suffering millions.

This was the vision. On a practical level, Martin gave the $50,000 prize to be shared amongst the various civil rights organisations in the United States.

What a long way he had come in the twenty-five years since he was told he must try on his shoes at the back of the shop out of sight of the white citizens of Atlanta! In Oslo, he was greeted by kings and princes. On his return to New York on 16th December, he was received by Mayor Wagner, Governor Rockefeller and Vice-President Hubert Humphrey. Even his home city of Atlanta – scene of his first humiliation as a negro – entertained him at a banquet for fifteen hundred people at the Dinkler Plaza Hotel. The guests were mixed black and white – unheard of in Atlanta until them.

When Martin rose to accept the city's gift to him of an inscribed Steuben bowl, he commented that all the ceremony was 'quite a contrast to what I face almost every day under the threat of death, and it's a fine contrast to have people say nice things. I wish I could stay on the mountain, but the valley calls me . . .'

12. A Season of Suffering

The particular valley that was calling Martin in January 1965 was Selma, Alabama (population 29,000, of whom 14,000 were whites and 15,000 were blacks. Only 150 of those blacks were registered to vote).

On 18th January, Martin, somewhat shaken by having been knocked about by a white rough earlier that day in his hotel lobby, led four hundred of his fellow negroes to the Selma Courthouse to register their vote. Sheriff Jim Clark met them at the door and told them that no registrars were on duty.

Martin said 'If they refuse to register us, we will appeal to Governor Wallace. If *he* doesn't listen, we will appeal to the legislature. If the legislature doesn't listen, we will dramatise the situation to arouse the Federal government by marching by the thousand to the places of registration. We must be willing to go to jail by the thousand.'

They did just that! On 1st February, when Martin led a march of negroes to the Courthouse to register, he was arrested along with seven hundred and seventy others, and the following day a further five hundred and fifty were arrested.

Martin begged that Congress would pass stronger legislation with regard to voting rights and that the Selma registrars could be ordered to work every day to get everybody registered who wanted it, but a Federal court order somewhat lamely instructed the registrars to work 'more often' than twice monthly. On 9th February, Martin, once more at liberty, met Vice-President Humphrey and the Attorney-General designate and was given a firm assurance that a strong voting Bill would be sent to Congress 'in the near future' – but that could be *any* time.

In the meantime, Sheriff Jim Clark was showing what *he* thought of the situation.

Sheriff Clark was a policeman in the 'Bull' Connor mould. He was a big man – 220 lbs (nearly 16 stone). He was forty-two years old and had the reputation of being the 'best-dressed Sheriff in the Black Belt'. He wore an outsize lapel button with the word 'NEVER' on it, in reply to the negroes' chant of 'We Shall Overcome'.

On February 9th, he and his officers, in cars and trucks, drove a hundred and sixty-five black youngsters at the trot for three miles, using electric cattle prods to keep them on the move.

One could almost have sympathised with the black community had they felt that the Sheriff's heart attack immediately afterwards (fortunately for him, not a serious one) was some form of 'judgment'. Instead, two hundred black youngsters knelt on the pavement before the Courthouse in Selma and prayed for the recovery of their persecutor!

The time had now come for Part 2 of Martin's plan to be put into practice: the appeal to Governor Wallace. Not that they had much hope of moving the Governor. He was notoriously unsympathetic and the whole state of Alabama had a poor record of registering black voters. Admittedly, the number had gone up from six thousand in 1947 to a hundred and ten thousand in 1964, but there were even now three hundred and seventy thousand unregistered negroes in the state. Still, it would be a good public relations exercise to march the fifty miles from Selma to Montgomery and to petition the Governor.

The march was fixed for Sunday, 7th March. The night before, Martin (who was not going to be able to accompany the march owing to commitments elsewhere) addressed the marchers at Brown Chapel. He explained the policy behind the march, stressed the need for orderliness and good humour, and warned the marchers that they would need courage:

> 'I can't promise you that it won't get you beaten. I can't promise you that it won't get your house bombed. I can't promise you won't get scarred up a bit. But we must stand up for what is right.'

In Martin's absence, Hosea Williams led the march. Five hundred marchers set out from Brown Chapel in quiet order, singing hymns and keeping in disciplined lines along U.S. Highway 80 towards Montgomery. But, just outside the town at Pettus Bridge, the marchers ran into an ambush. On the far side of the bridge, Alabama State Troopers blocked their way. Behind them, Sheriff Clark and a posse of vigilantes who had been in hiding closed off any chance of retreat. The marchers were given two minutes in which to disperse. But there was nowhere they could disperse to and, within minutes, they were being attacked by police in gas masks throwing tear gas canisters and by Sheriff Clark and his mounted vigilantes striking them down with cattle prods and clubs. Above the hubbub, Sheriff Clark was yelling 'Get those Goddam niggers!'

Seventeen marchers were seriously hurt and forty others needed hospital treatment. Doctors from New

York who had come to support the marchers were not allowed to treat the injured and it was not until the Chief of Police, Wilson Baker, intervened and managed to get the marchers into the safety of a church that Sheriff Clark could be persuaded to withdraw his mob.

Martin hurried back to Selma the following day and arranged to lead a second march on Tuesday, 9th March. It was not immodest on his part to realise that he was now of sufficient standing to attract the maximum amount of publicity to any demonstration he attended. And publicity – good publicity – was what the movement needed if it was to win over the hearts and minds of white America.

He had notable support from white America on this occasion: Rabbi Hirsch (Chief Rabbi of the Jewish Community in America); Monsignor George Gingras of the Catholic Church; Bishop John Wesley Lord of the Episcopal Church; the wives of a number of white Senators (the American near-equivalent of a British Member of Parliament). Support came from all over the United States. There were to be 'sympathy marches' held at the same time in Toronto and Detroit, each led by the leading citizens of the community.

The Government in Washington was worried. It was a scenario that would fire the imagination of the press, radio and television and that would stir the conscience of most Americans: on the one side, a small southern town showing itself to be outrageously prejudiced against its black citizens; on the other side, a courageous group of negroes, seeking peacefully to establish the most minimal rights; and a sadistic police force, which should have been upholding those rights, using instead brute force to support the oppressors. And if Dr. Martin Luther King, Jnr., minister of religion, Nobel Prize winner, undoubted leader of the black Civil Rights movement and the only man who not only advocated but seemed able by sheer force of personality to ensure *peaceful* protest – if such a man as he were to be injured or even killed in Selma, the White House and Justice Department were only too well aware of the upsurge of black protest that might follow. They tried to persuade Martin not to take part in the march but he was not prepared to give way, whatever the risks.

Once again the disciplined ranks of negroes left Selma by Highway 80. Once again, the march was halted at Pettus Bridge. On this occasion, however, instead of cattle prods and clubs, the march was confronted by one man – an officer of the Federal court who produced an injunction banning the march. The powers-that-be in Washington had moved fast to stop any chance of a confrontation.

Martin was always careful (except in that one exceptional case in Birmingham) to obey the law, so there was no alternative but to return to Selma. First of all, though, he called upon the marchers to kneel in prayer, after which they returned peacefully to their homes. Some of the white supporters, however, were not so fortunate. Three white priests who had come to join Martin on the march were brutally set upon by some of the white extremists of Selma. The Reverend James Reeb of Boston was so badly beaten around the head that he died.

The nation was shocked – but, then, it had been shocked many times before over atrocities arising out of the southern whites' hatred of negroes but nothing happened. By the following day, some new sensation would have replaced the Reverend Reeb's murder in the headlines.

In Selma, both black and white members of the community wanted to hold a prayer meeting for the dead man outside the Courthouse but permission for this was refused. The meeting was held in the town stadium the following day.

George Wallace, the Governor of Alabama, was summoned to Washington to explain to President Johnson why such violence should be condoned. Wallace tried to lay the blame on a small group of trouble-makers but the President made it clear that his sympathies lay with the demonstrators.

On Monday, March 15th, President Johnson addressed Congress to announce that a Bill granting Voting Rights to negroes would be laid before the house on the following Wednesday. Among other things, the Bill would remove the literacy test that had up till now prevented many negroes from registering as voters. It had not just been a test of a negro's ability to read and write – sometimes the literacy test had taken the form of interpreting the Constitution of the United States – something which probably the Registrar himself could not do!

'What happened in Selma,' said the President, 'is part of a far larger movement which reaches into every section and state of America. It is the effort of American negroes to secure for themselves the full blessings of American life.

Their cause must be our cause, too. Because it's not just Negroes, but really all of us who must overcome the crippling legacy of bigotry and injustice. And we . . . shall . . . overcome.'

Two days later, on the day the Voting Bill was to go before Congress, Judge Johnson lifted the injunction on the march to Montgomery and gave his authority for it to go ahead. Moreover, he specifically forbade Governor Wallace, Sheriff Clark of any other state official to interfere with it.

The march that took place on Sunday, 21st March, was very different from the previous abortive one Martin had led only twelve days before. Only three hundred were to be allowed to march on the highway but they were protected by no fewer than four thousand Federal troops! There was an Army Field Hospital set up to deal with casualties. Members of the FBI infiltrated the vast crowds that came from all over the States to cheer the marchers on their way. In fact, the 'protection' was almost too effective for the drone of Army helicopters overhead almost drowned the speeches, and the accompanying TV trucks raised dust that enveloped and choked the marchers! In addition to the thousands of supporters for the march, there was also a hostile white element who waved banners reading 'Martin Luther Coon', 'Bye Bye, Blackbird' and other insulting slogans.

It took five days to march the fifty miles between Selma and Montgomery and by the end of that time the three hundred marchers had swelled to thirty thousand. It was a bit different from the first, experimental bus boycott in Montgomery ten years before – but no different in the dusty answer the marchers received. Despite President Johnson's words to Governor Wallace, when Martin led the thirty thousand marchers down Dexter Avenue to Montgomery's capitol building to present their petition, he found the office closed and the Governor 'away'.

Moreover, in addition to an outbreak of bombings throughout the state, a young white woman, Mrs. Viola Liuzzo, who had volunteered to use her car to get the marchers home, was shot in the head and killed by white vigilantes. The tragedy left five small children without a mother.

'If physical death is the price some must pay to save us and our white brothers from eternal death of the spirit,' Martin said on TV that night, 'then no sacrifice could be more redemptive.'

Jesus had said: 'There is no greater love than this, that a man should lay down his life for his friends' (John 15.13).

13.   Slum Clearance

Martin would not have been blamed had he given up his work for Civil Rights that spring of 1965. Thanks to President Johnson, he had gained great advances *in law* for the benefit of the negro – over voting, education, segregated services and the like. The fact that the southern states still defied the Federal law was at times hard to bear but it must surely only be a matter of time before they had to conform. Persecution and oppression and violence had been part of the southern white's treatment of the negro for so long that it would take years rather than months to change them but he had faith that freedom and equality *would* one day come to the black millions of the United States.

He was thirty-six years old and had had to spend long periods of his twelve-year married life away from his wife and four children. He had been imprisoned on numerous occasions and was constantly in danger. It cannot have been easy for Coretta to make her young family understand *why* their Daddy was in prison when he had done nothing wrong. The children, too, must sometimes have suffered from the taunts of their schoolmates. But Coretta had promised to support Martin to the full, whatever direction his life should take, and this love and loyalty must have sustained Martin through many difficult days.

He was co-pastor with his father of Atlanta's Ebenezer Baptist Church but was not often there to care for his flock. He had every excuse to leave the struggle in other hands and seek the comfort of anonymity.

But a relentless sense of destiny drove him on. He knew that he had been called by God to be a very special, peace-loving leader of his people and he would not shirk the responsibility, no matter what the cost. Negroes in Montgomery at the time of the first bus boycott, when he had been repeatedly vilified and arrested by the white authorities, had called him affectionately 'Little Lord Jesus'. While Martin would be the first person to repudiate such a description, the onlooker could perhaps see in him a resolution that drew its inspiration from Christ. St. Luke's Gospel (9.51) tells how Jesus 'set his face resolutely towards Jerusalem', knowing the suffering that awaited him there. Martin, with similar courage but only a vague foreboding, now set his face to the next phase of his mission.

While he was grateful to President Johnson for the action he had taken in Congress to improve the lot of the negro, he was bitterly opposed to the costly Viet Nam war in which the President had embroiled the United States. He spoke out against it – with the result, sadly, of undermining the good relationship he had established with the President.

On August 6th, 1965, he was invited by the President to be present along with other negro leaders at the historic signing into law of the Voting Rights Bill, but that was the end of their special understanding. Later that month, Martin publicly criticised the Viet Nam war – an act which President Johnson found unforgivable.

But what else could Martin do?

As a Christian and as a minister of the church, he *must*

denounce war. As a holder of the Nobel Prize for Peace, he *must* work for peace between nations. As a black Civil Rights leader, he *must* attack a war which was squandering billions of dollars that could better be spent on the relief of poverty at home.

In an article in the *Chicago Defender* in January, 1966, Martin wrote:

'I am an American . . . and I have construed love of country as synonymous with love of democracy, justice and peace. The destruction of Viet Nam villages proves that the U.S. still believes might is right. It would be heresy for the American black to demand the full measure of human dignity for himself while ignoring its denial to others elsewhere.'

This article further alienated Martin from the President and, although he had to be invited to the White House occasionally for conferences on civil rights, he was from now on pointedly ignored at these meetings.

Moreover, the depth of his argument and of his thinking was not always appreciated by his fellow blacks, either. Many criticised him and said he should stick to purely domestic issues. At least when many of his own people turned against him, he was comforted by Coretta's whole-hearted support. The young woman who had put aside her desire for active resistance when she married Martin had over the years become a convinced pacifist.

The issue of the war was pushed to one side, however, as race riots erupted in the northern United States, particularly at Watts, the black ghetto of Los Angeles, where disorders lasted for four days. In that short time there were thirty-four deaths, over a thousand injuries, four thousand arrests and damage to property estimated at over forty million dollars.

Martin decided he had been spending too much effort over the plight of negroes in the south and had been blinded to the hideous economic conditions of blacks in the north. Negroes in the old 'Yankee' states of the American Civil War had for years had the vote and had been able to move freely about their towns and cities but this appearance of freedom masked the fact that they were in reality no better off than their southern brothers. They had only the poorest jobs and the poorest housing. The black ghettos of New York and Chicago were probably worse than the poorest black areas of the south.

Martin spoke out in condemnation of negro violence but said that some blame must be attached to those who contributed to the poverty and dreadful conditions of the black slums.

In January 1966, he went to Chicago to see for himself the slums in which one third of that city's population lived. He planned a campaign that would be directed against the landlords who refused to carry out repairs to slum properties. If need be, he would call for a rent strike.

It was not easy to drum up support for his campaign. There was growing militancy among blacks throughout the United States. 'We Shall Overcome', the anthem of the Civil Rights marchers, became 'We Shall Over-*Run*' when chanted by 'Black Power' followers. A new black leader had arisen in the south – Stokeley Carmichael – whose declared creed was 'Power is the only thing respected in this world, and we must get it at any cost.'

Carmichael was leading disturbances down south in Mississippi so Martin hurried there to plead with him and the demonstrators to follow the way of *non*-violence. But it seemed that his influence was waning. Young blacks who only knew him for his 'I Have a Dream' speech and were unaware of the considerable gains he had already achieved, were impatient for results. They wanted the dream to become an immediate reality.

On Sunday, 10th July 1966, Martin addressed a big crowd at Soldiers Field, Chicago. Just as the Martin Luther for whom he was named had in 1517 nailed to the door of Wittenburg Church his list of contradictions of the Pope, so on this day Martin nailed *his* eight-point demand to the door of the civic centre. It called for improvements in housing and jobs, and the removal of discrimination.

The following day he met Mayor Daley, the tough leading citizen of Chicago. The meeting was not a success and some negroes in the city rioted in protest at the failure of the talks. They met again and this time Mayor Daley agreed to some concessions: on access to parks and open spaces. He promised that swimming pools would be built for negroes to use. But to a request that the actions of the police be looked into, Mayor Daley gave an uncompromising refusal.

Again, negro disappointment expressed itself in criticism of Martin. Non-violence was inefficient and out-of-date, he was told. Today's conditions called for positive action. The whites needed 'shaking up'. One day of riots would have a more positive effect than a whole year of peaceful demonstrations. All he had achieved was 'Promises'. Martin responded vigorously:

'Even if every Negro in the United States comes to think that Negroes ought to riot,' he told the Chicago civil rights workers, 'I'm going to stand as that lone voice and say, "it's impractical, it's unsound, and we'll never get our own way that way".'

To indicate his close identification with the current campaign, Martin moved Coretta and the children that summer from their comfortable home in Atlanta to a slum apartment in one of the worst areas of Chicago. He was dismayed at the effect it had on them:

'Their tempers flared,' he wrote in *Where Do We Go From Here*? 'and they sometimes reverted to almost infantile behaviour. As riots raged around them outside, I realised that the crowded flat in which we lived was about to produce an emotional explosion in my own family. It was just too hot, too crowded, too devoid of creative forms of recreation.'

Here was a demonstration on his own doorstep of the point he had been making about the riots at Watts the previous summer: that violence germinated in squalid conditions and that those who permitted or even encouraged the squalid conditions must bear some responsibility for the demonstrators.

When he arrived to address a meeting at Marquette Park on 5th August, he was jeered at by hundreds of white protestors. One of them hurled a rock at him and knocked him to the ground but he picked himself up and, though shaken, proceeded with his address. 'I have to do this,' he said, 'to expose myself to danger, to bring this hate into the open.'

Police prevented further violence but Martin and his followers had to run the gauntlet of several thousand jeering white hecklers when they marched to the offices of the biggest firm of estate agents in the city and knelt in prayer in the road outside. Martin said afterwards that he had endured much opposition in his time but that that day in Chicago showed more hatred and hostility than he had experienced anywhere up to that time.

The following week, wherever and whenever the marches took place, rioters attacked marchers and police indiscriminately. They would chant:

'I wish I were an Alabama trooper.
That is what I would truly like to be.
I wish I were an Alabama trooper
'Cause then I could kill the niggers legally.'

The tensions in the city were extreme, the weight of
hatred overwhelming. So much violence, so much
intolerance, so much raw savagery – could this be
happening in the United States of America in 1966?

On Wednesday, August 17th, Martin and his colleagues
had another session of talks with Mayor Daley and
representatives of the property firms. The negroes pressed
for penalties against estate agents who showed discrimination against coloured applicants. After eight hours, the
meeting broke up with no agreement on anything except
the date of the next meeting.

That night Mayor Daley went on television to appeal for
calm. Certainly calm was needed. Whenever there was a
demonstration, it seemed to bring out the most fanatical of
white opponents. The sale of firearms to whites had
increased alarmingly (In America, anyone can buy a gun
without having a licence as is required in Britain). Most
worrying of all, Lincoln Rockwell, the leader of the
American Nazi Party, had arrived in Chicago and that
boded ill for the negroes.

Amidst all this violence and threat of more, there was on
this occasion no intervention by Washington as there had
been in Selma the year before. Martin was out of favour
with the President. Also, unlike Governor Wallace of
Alabama, Mayor Daley was a well-respected member of
the Democratic party and therefore was unlikely to be
'pressured' by Washington.

The Mayor obtained an injunction from the court
limiting marches to one per day and then only after

twenty-four hours' notice had been given. No more than five hundred people could take part in any march and such a march would only be permitted during certain limited hours. Many people were watching to see whether Martin would violate the injunction but he decided not to. He gave a week's notice that he proposed to lead a march on Sunday, 28th August, to Cicero, one of Chicago's most exclusive white residential areas. He was heartened because, for the first time, a number of the young black militants with whom he had spent a great deal of time talking and explaining, agreed to support him in a non-violent demonstration.

Mayor Daley was really alarmed at the prospect of the Cicero march and begged Martin to abandon it. The National Guard and State Police were placed on alert. At the last moment, however, a 'summit meeting' was called between black and white leaders and a compromise was reached regarding more open housing, more money for mortgages and other benefits for negroes. The march to Cicero was postponed.

When Martin thankfully returned to Atlanta with his family, what could he consider he had achieved in Chicago? Not a miracle – but then, he did not expect miracles. His demonstrations were intended primarily to draw attention to particular problems affecting the black community. Any concessions won at the time were a bonus; it was his policy usually to leave the local civil rights leaders to build on the foundations he had laid.

In Chicago there had been some small advances, although, so far, the vast problem of slum living conditions and poor jobs had barely been touched upon. The big success was that Mayor Daley – one of the toughest and most powerful mayors in the United States – had been brought to concede that there *was* a problem in his city and that the problem needed urgent attention.

'I have a dream that the children of slaves and slave-owners will one day live in brotherhood...'

Would he, Martin, see the dream realised in his lifetime?

14.   Decline

Ever since his Nobel Prize acceptance speech in Oslo in December 1964, Martin had developed a wider vision of his purpose. All that he had read of Jesus' message in the Gospels, all that he had studied from Gandhi's writings and actions in India, combined to convince him that his concern should be for a wider issue than the black/white struggle, important though that was. Chicago made him realise that his purposes could not be achieved without 'a reconstruction of society, a revolution of values'. It was no longer a question of improving the jobs and bargaining power of negroes alone; it must extend to all the poor and oppressed, of whatever colour – and how could this be achieved when the United States was embroiled in a bloody and costly conflict on the other side of the Pacific?

He was not popular in taking a stand for peace, either with white Americans or with black. America was still too newly in the war to be sickened by its atrocities or by the demoralising effect it was having on the country's armed forces. Violence was the prevailing mood of America. 'Black Power' characters had become the cult figures of press and TV. Riots were more newsworthy than peaceful marches.

Despite his fading popularity with the public, Martin led a big peace march in Chicago on 25th March 1967 and on 4th April made an impassioned plea at New York's

Riverside Church for an end to the war in Viet Nam. The burden of his speeches was the danger of the conflict erupting into a Third World War. He felt that the horrors perpetrated by U.S. Forces in Viet Nam would 'explode at home and destroy the dream and possibility of a decent America.'

On 15th April, he was one of the leaders of a huge demonstration for peace when a hundred and twenty-five thousand people marched from Central Park in New York to the United Nations building. In his speech, Martin deplored the indiscriminate devastation of Viet Nam by Americans:

'The people,' he said, 'watch as we poison their water, as we kill a million acres of their crops . . . They must weep as the bulldozers roar through their areas preparing to destroy the precious trees. They wander into the hospitals with at least twenty casualties from American firepower for one Vietcong-inflicted injury'.

He deplored the ever upward spiralling investment in the war that contributed to the economic destitution of whole sections of the community and consequently to racial unrest.

It was no suprise when the summer of 1967 erupted into the most violent race riots the United States had yet experienced. Fifty cities were torn apart. July 23rd left forty-three dead and five thousand injured in Detroit alone.

Despite all the promises, all the laws passed, the actual improvements in negro conditions so far barely scratched the surface of the problem. Negro discontent was as bitter as ever.

Martin's depression deepened. Had he achieved *anything* for all his efforts, all his speeches, all his suffering? It was with a deep sense of hopelessness that in

October he once again found himself in prison – this time arising from the charge of demonstrating without a valid permit for which he had been granted bail in Birmingham in 1963! Even his prison sentences were no longer the cause for world-wide protest. The Civil Rights issue was yesterday's news; Martin Luther King was yesterday's man.

He was very tired, very low in spirit, but he would not give up.

In December 1967, he outlined in Atlanta an idea that seemed to crystallise his thinking. He suggested a Poor People's March on Washington to take place in April of the following year. It would not just be a demonstration by negroes but by *all* America's oppressed minorities. There would be Puerto Ricans and Mexicans and Red Indians and 'poor whites' of whom there were all too many in America.

In January, 1968, he called a meeting of ministers in Miami, Florida, to obtain official sanction for the march and to begin planning.

By February 12th, a 'master plan' for the Poor People's March had been drawn up. Three thousand demonstrators would be drawn from Roxbury, the ghetto area of Boston; from Chicago's Lawndale community; from Mississippi and from West Virginia. They would camp out in Washington for three months from 20th April and would lobby Congress and various Government departments. They would press for twelve billion dollars to be set aside for improvements in the conditions of the poor. The racial struggle had moved on to become a class struggle.

It would be a good time for a protest march because, once again, 1968 was an Election year. Both Robert Kennedy and Senator McCarthy were standing against

President Johnson as Democratic candidates for the Presidency. Both were against the Viet Nam war so Martin's stand on the war was 'respectable' again. He continued to speak out against it and also to protest that the President had failed to see that the very important legislation he had pushed through Congress on behalf of negroes was carried out in practice.

Martin was even himself invited to stand as a candidate for the Presidency but declined to do so. Rewards and status were not important to him. As he had said in a sermon in his church in Atlanta on 4th February, even the Nobel Prize was not important.

He said that, when he died 'I'd like somebody to say that day . . . that Martin Luther King Jnr. tried to love somebody . . . I want you to be able to say that day that I did try to feed the hungry. I want you to be able to say that day that I did try in my life to clothe the naked . . . And I want you to say that I tried to love and serve humanity.'

It was almost as if he knew that not much of life remained to him. However, it was not physical death that he feared, but spiritual despair – and he was very near to that in those first months of 1968.

15.   Free at Last!

There was to be no time for brooding about failure.

In February 1968, trouble flared in Memphis, Tennessee, over the town's thirteen hundred sanitation workers – 'dustmen', they would be called in Britain. This was one of the least desirable jobs in the community and mostly it was carried out by blacks on a very low wage – a lower wage than whites doing the same work. In addition, working conditions were terrible. The only rest rooms provided were for white workers only; blacks had to take their time off in the streets; had to eat their lunch in the streets; even had to relieve themselves in the streets – and in so doing run the risk of being arrested for causing a public nuisance!

Dissatisfaction and resentment had been simmering for months but was triggered into protest when two negro workers were accidentally crushed to death by the automatic compressor of their truck. At the end of the week, white workers in the dead mens' 'gang' were given full wages whereas black members of the same 'gang' had money deducted from the hours the whole gang had missed on the day of the accident.

Martin was hurriedly invited to lead a protest march on Thursday, 28th March. The demonstration had not been properly planned and Martin had been delayed so that he only arrived at the last moment before the march and had no time to check the details. The march quickly broke up in chaos and sporadic violence. 'Black Power' representatives moved in to take over the march and in the ensuing riots, a sixteen-year-old boy was killed, fifty people were injured and a hundred and twenty were arrested.

Because he had been present, Martin was blamed for the failure of the demonstration. Adam Clayton Powell in New York called him 'Martin *Loser* King'. This added to Martin's depression. Could no-one appreciate that without his witness for peace, the violence of the past ten years would have been far, far worse?

He immediately announced that he would lead another march the following Friday. This time the march would be carefully organised to avoid extreme elements taking part. He himself tackled a young black militant group called 'The Young Invaders' and persuaded them that demonstrations *must* be peaceful.

On March 31st, he was in Washington where he had been invited to preach the Passion Sunday sermon in the cathedral. He spoke about racism and poverty and about the Poor People's March planned for three weeks ahead. It would not be an empty 'histrionic gesture', he promised.

He went back to Atlanta to see Coretta and the children, then flew to Memphis on 3rd April to put the final touches to the plans for the protest march. There was a long delay before the plane left and the captain of the aircraft announced to the passengers that the delay had been caused by a search for a bomb on board; they had to be extra careful when carrying Dr. Martin Luther King.

Martin and his party had booked accommodation at the Lorraine Motel in Memphis. All their rooms opened onto a balcony which ran the length of the back of the hotel, facing the gardens of the houses in South Main Street.

On that Wednesday evening, Martin was to have

addressed an assembly at Mason Temple. It was pouring with rain. He was very tired and still deeply depressed. He did not think that many people would turn out to hear him in such weather, so he asked his loyal friend, Ralph Abernathy, to address the meeting in his place.

When Ralph reached the church, it was obvious that the only person the big crowd wanted to hear was Martin. He phoned the Motel and Martin dragged himself down to the rally.

It was one of the most moving speeches of his life, though people who were there said he seemed nervous, at times almost trance-like. As he neared the end of his address, it was as if Martin knew that his end was very near:

'... Only when it is dark enough can you see the stars ... I see God working in this period of the twentieth century ... Something is happening in our world ...

Like anybody I would like to live ... But I'm not concerned about that now. I just want to do God's will! He's allowed me to go up to the mountain, and I've looked over – and I've seen the Promised Land. I may not get there with you, but I want you to know, tonight, that we as a people will get to the Promised Land!'

The next day, 4th April, the day before the proposed march, Martin seemed in better spirits. When two officers of the local court arrived at the Motel to serve on him an injunction forbidding the march, he seemed almost unconcerned. In any event, that Thursday was to be a 'free' day. He had talks with various black leaders and, again, with the young black militants. He and Ralph had been invited out to supper that evening and were looking forward to a promised highly-spiced southern meal of 'soul' food.

Just before 6 o'clock, they were on the balcony, joking with the Reverend Andrew Young and the Reverend Jesse Jackson and other friends in the courtyard below. Ralph went back into his room to collect his jacket. At 6.01 p.m., there was a single shot and Martin collapsed across the balcony, half his jaw blasted away by the violence of the explosion. Andy Young tore up the stairs. Ralph burst from his room and bent over Martin. There was a look of surprise on Martin's face; Ralph could not be sure whether or not he was still alive. Andrew Young was holding his wrist and thought he could detect a faint pulse.

There was shouting and confusion at the Motel. Police erupted from all over the place – they had apparently been keeping surveillance on the Motel, though whether to see what Martin was doing or to forestall any trouble is not clear. There were firemen from the Fire Station opposite, people from other rooms.

An ambulance arrived within minutes. When it reached Memphis hospital, a team of doctors was standing by, called into readiness by radio. There was to be no panic at the hospital as there had apparently been when President Kennedy was shot.

The team worked on Martin for an hour – a neuro-surgeon, a chest surgeon, a general surgeon, a lung specialist, a kidney specialist – but all knew that their work was only 'going through the motions'. Martin had died the instant the bullet hit him.

But who had fired the shot? And why?

It was soon apparent that the shot had come from the back of a seedy rooming house at 422½ South Main Street and investigation showed that a man armed with a rifle had hired Room 5B whose bathroom overlooked the balcony of the Motel, only two hundred feet away. The police even found a chair in position and the curtain drawn back to give the best view of the balcony.

But *who* was the man? And *why* had he killed?

There began the biggest manhunt in American history. It took police the length and breadth of the United States, to Canada and to Europe. It resulted in the arrest on 8th June, 1968 at London Airport of one James Earl Ray and in his eventual conviction for the murder.

But why? Was he a hired assassin or had he killed for his own reasons?

There were many and varied theories. Some said the murder was planned by black militants disaffected with Martin's stand for peace – but, if so, why wait until his fortunes were in decline? Some said it was a 'contract' put out by Southern whites who hated his unremitting campaign against segregation – but why wait until the main thrust of his campaign had moved from the black/white issues to the bigger one of world poverty? Some said it was the work of the FBI because Martin was an embarrassment to the Government. The FBI had certainly been using less than admirable methods to detract from Martin's high reputation – but why wait until *after* President Johnson had announced (as he had done three weeks before) that he was not going to stand for a second term as President? Some said it was the work of the CIA because Martin was, they said, a Communist; others said it was the work of Communists, part of a series of killings that started with President Kennedy and continued with the assassination of Robert Kennedy only two months after Martin's death. Was James Earl Ray a fanatic who felt he was expressing the wish of the American people in killing a man whom so many reviled?

The court eventually decided that Ray had had a personal grudge against negroes in general and that Martin was killed as a symbol. It seemed a thin story for Ray had spent most of his adult life in prison and had had little contact with negroes. Perhaps the court's decision was in itself a cover-up, perhaps not.

But what difference did it make, the 'who' or the 'why'? A great and good man had been struck down with cruel suddenness at the age of thirty-eight. He was five years older than Jesus was when He was crucified; he was a little under half the age of Mahatma Gandhi when he was assassinated. All three died in the cause of love for mankind, for the brotherhood of man, for its redemption from the sins of cruelty and hatred and intolerance.

Martin would not have enjoyed his funeral service. He had always said that, when he died, he wanted a simple, brief service. Instead, the world's press and TV covered an almost State occasion attended by the Vice-President of the United States; by the chief candidates in the forthcoming Presidential elections; by fifty members of the House of Representatives; by thirty Senators; by Mayors from cities all over the United States – by so many to whom he had been a thorn in the flesh while alive and who now, at his death, recognised him as a martyr.

There were foreign dignitaries and private citizens who had respected him. There were Coretta and the four children, and his father and mother and brother and sister, and Ralph Abernathy, who had all loved him.

The coffin was borne on a cart drawn by a mule – symbolic of the negro's position in American society from which Martin had struggled to lift him.

The white-walled airy Ebenezer Baptist Church in Atlanta was packed. The big rose window depicting Christ at Gethsemane seemed to symbolise much of Martin's own agonies and submission to the purpose to which he felt called. The choir, robed in white and green, sang Martin's favourite hymns. Daddy King led the long, emotional service, tears streaming down his wrinkled cheeks.

One of the eulogies was spoken by Robert Kennedy, Attorney-General of the United States – symbolic of the heights to which Martin Luther King's dedication and persistence had lifted him.

His had been a rare personality. He had been intelligent, courageous, eloquent and loving. His murder had shocked the world. Perhaps this latest explosion of violence, to be followed so soon by the assassination of Robert Kennedy, shocked the American people into sense for very soon afterwards, popular opinion began to repudiate the obscenity of the Viet Nam war.

As far as Civil Rights were concerned, there was still a long way to go before all Martin's aims would be achieved. There was scattered violence throughout the seventies, and constant legislation and protest and appeals over voting rights and schools and housing – but if Martin had felt in his day that he took one step forward only to slip back two, the seventies brought two steps forward for negroes and only one back.

How proud Martin would have been had he been alive in 1977 to see President Carter appoint as United States Ambassador to the United Nations that same Reverend Andrew Young who had felt for Martin's pulse on the balcony of the Lorraine Motel that fatal day in Memphis. Young was the first negro ever to hold US Ambassador status. How Martin would have rejoiced in 1983 to learn that for the first time a negro, Harold Washington, had been elected Mayor of the great city of Chicago. He had only been able to work in faith towards such gains.

'And what is faith?' St. Paul asked in his Letter to the

Hebrews (11.1). 'Faith gives substance to our hopes, and makes us certain of realities we do not see.'

Dr. Martin Luther King, Jnr. is buried in Southview Cemetery, Atlanta. There is no statue, no elaborate memorial – just a modest marble block on which are inscribed the words:

'Free at last. Free at last.
Thank God Almighty,
I'm Free at last.'

He had fought a good fight, he had finished his course, he had kept the faith.

Other Marshalls Paperbacks

FROM PRISON TO PULPIT

Vic Jackopson

'Father died when he was a year old.
Mother deserted.
Family broken up.
Failed fostering experiment.
Above average intelligence.
One more chance.'

Vic was used to probation officers pleading his case in court. He had learnt to take care of himself early on in the orphanage, but years of fighting, stealing and burgling had brought him to the end of the line.

'God, if you are there, you've got ten days to change my life and if you haven't done it by then you've copped it.'

Vic prayed, God acted. It wasn't always easy from then on, but living by the grace of God rather than by his own fists Vic found a new inner strength and security. Instead of taking from others he now teaches and lives the new life Christ brings into the hearts of men and women.

LOVE IN 'BOMB CITY'

Ben Forde with Chris Spencer

Ben Forde, a Belfast CID detective, shares from his personal experience his conviction that amid the sectarian hatred there is a powerful force of love at work—a love which is bringing forgiveness and healing in a province notorious for its bitterness and division.

He also discusses Northern Ireland from the wider perspective of God's sovereign plan, seeking to make sense of the suffering with which he comes into contact almost every day in the course of his work. He asks: Has God forsaken Northern Ireland? Is he passing judgment on the sins of the people? Or is he actively preparing Ulster for a specific role in future world events? And what of the terrorism? Will the troubles in Northern Ireland ever end? What is the real purpose behind the violence? And how can countries like Britain and America, where terrorism is only just beginning to rear its ugly head, benefit from the painful experiences of Northern Ireland?

Love in 'Bomb City' provides some stimulating answers.

WHERE CHRIST IS STILL TORTURED

Richard Wurmbrand

'Except for the Bible, nothing has shaken me like Wurmbrand.' *Tortured for Christ*. 'It is the message of the century—Even more: it is the most powerful *Acts of the Martyrs* since the persecution of Christians by Nero.'

Kurt Koch

In this book Richard Wurmbrand brings the story up to date. Persecution continues to tighten its grip on infant Christian Churches in lands ruled by atheists and tyrants. It is only the power of the Holy Spirit which enables them to survive and flourish in the face of discrimination, oppression, torture and murder. What is the response of the cossetted Western church? Does it understand what is happening? Satanic forces are working to stifle Christian witness in the world today, and Christians in the West need to be able to recognize and fight their enemy.

MY ROUGH DIAMOND

Doris Lemon with Anne Tyler

'Not all women have husbands who turn out to be viciously tempered, drunkards, or even convicts—but some women do. It can be a nightmare to be married to such a man: the isolation of it, the shame, the loneliness you feel. And fear! Fear for yourself, for the children. How do you cope? Where do you get the stamina and endurance from?

I've written this book so as to share with you my experiences—and the lessons I learned from them—and to tell you that God is able to make all the difference.

Of course, it was marvellous when Fred became a Christian. It was the start of a whole new life for us. But maybe your husband isn't a Christian, and you're all alone and fed up. That's how it was for me for many years. Here's the lessons I learned from my marriage, and not only how I learned to live with, but also, how to help my rough diamond . . .'

Doris has been married to her husband, Fred, for twenty-seven years. Fred Lemon's story is told in *Breakout*, and he has also written *Going Straight* and *Breakthrough*.

FREED FOR LIFE

Rita Nightingale

'Today, at round 11 am I got a twenty-year prison sentence. It didn't come as a shock, but it certainly came as a surprise. I was expecting over thirty . . .'

Prison Diary, 9 December 1977

Rita's sentence in Bangkok for drug-smuggling caused world-wide headlines. But the **real** story is how she became a Christian whilst in a Thai prison and how her life was transformed.

ORDER! ORDER!

Ramon Hunston

A scene in Parliament today. The Speaker, resplendent in his robes, subdues the unruly backbenchers . . . 'Order! Order!'

George Thomas now holds one of the highest posts in the land. His rise from the childhood poverty of the Welsh mining valleys, living with four brothers and sisters in a tiny Rhondda 'underhouse', is a remarkable testimony to his character, determination, and above all to his Christian faith. He explains to Ramon Hunston how it has weathered both the storms of doubt and the pressures of holding down one of the most demanding jobs which can be imagined. He relates it to his socialist commitment and his actions and attitudes in public life. As he says of himself—'It is amazing what God can do with a lad from the Rhondda with a patch on his trousers.'

TOWARDS CONFIRMATION

John Eddison

Why should I be confirmed? What does it mean?

This book explains how confirmation is a sign that you intend to walk as a Christian, and that God has accepted you as one of His Sons. It outlines the basics of the Christian faith and how it affects your day-to-day life. It helps you to understand one of the most important events in your life.